POLITICAL CHANGE IN VIEW OF THE THEORY OF CHANGE AND BALANCED, HARMONIOUS UNION OF THE PRIVATE INTEREST AND THE PUBLIC INTEREST

Mun Chang Koo

University Press of America,® Inc.
Lanham · Boulder · New York · Toronto · Plymouth, UK

Copyright © 2010 by
University Press of America,® Inc.
4501 Forbes Boulevard
Suite 200
Lanham, Maryland 20706
UPA Acquisitions Department (301) 459-3366

Estover Road
Plymouth PL6 7PY
United Kingdom

All rights reserved
Printed in the United States of America
British Library Cataloging in Publication Information Available

Library of Congress Control Number: 2010925378
ISBN: 978-0-7618-5125-7 (paperback : alk. paper)
eISBN: 978-0-7618-5126-4

∞™ The paper used in this publication meets the minimum
requirements of American National Standard for Information
Sciences—Permanence of Paper for Printed Library Materials,
ANSI Z39.48-1992

Dedication

Until this theory was studied and published as a book, my parents, who helped in many ways, were still sweating in the farm field—even in their eighties. I dedicate this book to them. I also devote it to the spirit of the departed former president of the Korean Philosophy Association, Chong Ho Bae and departed former director of the Toegaehak Study Institute, Dong Chun Lee.

1994
Mun Chang Koo
(具 文 藏)

Contents

1. Research into Theories of Political Change ... 1
   The Goal and Necessity of Research ... 1
   The Scope and Method of Research ... 2

2. Theories of Political Change ... 5
   Definition of Political Change ... 5
   The Principle of Change in Modernization Theory ... 7
   The Principle of Change in Conflict Theory ... 10
   The Principle of Change-in-Balance Theory ... 18

3. The Theory of Change (易理) ... 29
   Definition of Chou I (周易) ... 29
   Theory of Tai Chi (太極) and Yin Yang (陰陽) ... 34
   Theory of Ho Tu (河圖), Lo Shu (洛書)
      and the Origination of Wu Hang (五行) ... 44
   Change Theory of Chou I ... 53
      Creation ... 53
      Yang Pien Yin Hua (陽變陰化) ... 61
      Cycling Order ... 69
      Harmonious Unification ... 72
      Balance ... 84
      Stability ... 89
   Problems of the Theory of Change ... 92

4. Political Change in the View of the Theory of Change (Chou I) ... 109
   The Concept of Ta Hsiao (大小) ... 109
   Ta Hsiao Reaction and Political Change ... 113
      Creation ... 118
      Yang Pien Yin Hua ... 121

Cycling Order	121
Harmonious Unification	122
Balance	128
Stability	130
The Theory of Change as a Theory of Political Change	132
5. Search for the Pattern of the Political Change	137
The Meanings of Searching New Theory	137
Definition of the BHUPP (Ta Hsiao Chun Ho, 大小均合)	138
Conflict Theory and the BHUPP	141
Ideological Conflict and the BHUPP	143
Labor Disputes and the BHUPP	145
The Relationship between Civilian and Government and the BHUPP	148
6. Conclusion	151
Bibliography	155

Chapter 1

Research into Theories of Political Change

The Goal and Necessity of Research

The theory of social development has expanded and become an increasingly important aspect of political science. Early researchers in the field of political development focused on the process of political change from absolute monarchy. Thereafter, they studied the process of institutionalization of the political system in its movement toward parliamentary democracy. They saw this as evolutionary. Recently, the study of third-world societies has revealed that the Western model of parliamentary democracy does not easily take hold in the third world.

Recently, political scientists have focused their studies on improved functioning of political systems through differentiation and specialization rather than on the influence of Western parliamentary democracy.[1]

In contrast, dialectic theory has been used to analyze political development. Dialectical materialism, according to the historicism of Karl Marx, is a typical example. The Marxist-Leninist school looked for causes of development in the conflict between social classes. Because they attached so much importance to conflict, they encouraged it as a means of hastening development. Societies following that lead became characterized by conflict. When it became clear that achieving the ideal society through conflict was an impractical dream, most analysts started to condemn that theory. But dialectical theory, once widely disseminated, took root in the politico-academic community. Therefore, modern political scientists still tend to use conflict, as well as evolutionary theory, in their analysis of the dynamics of change and modernization.

Even though political scientists still use both evolutionary theory and conflict theory, the subject of political change is a relatively underdeveloped field. The final direction of that study is ambiguous, and both the process of political change and the principle of dynamic change are still emerging.

While Western studies of political change proceed along the previously stated lines, this study focuses on the *Book of Change* (Chou I, 周易) which explains change in all things and affairs, and which has dominated oriental thought in this field for more than three thousand years. The aim of the present work is to analyze and arrange its theory of change (易理) and to apply it to political reality. Therefore, this book analyzes and summarizes the theories of change and applies those theories to political change. From that process it develops the theories of political change and tests their usefulness in the real world. The result is to develop and present a new theory of political change.

The Scope and Method of Research

The aim of this research is to introduce a theory of political change based on analysis of the general theory of change. But because the theory of change includes all the theories of the change of all things and affairs since the beginning of the universe—the accumulated knowledge of thousands of years—its scope is so wide that it is impossible to analyze as part of a thesis. This is especially true since ancient oriental scholarship is not differentiated. Scholarship in all fields of sciences is lumped together. This makes it impossible to analyze the whole of oriental sciences as a single research subject. Therefore, this thesis focuses only on change theories which are applicable to the theory of the political change and applies those theories to political change and its causes and direction, especially the principle of change action. Not only the *Book of Change* (I Ching, 易經 Chou I, 周易) but also many other books and articles are cited in this study. *Chou I* is one of the nine books (四書五經) of scholarships which constitute a huge system of Confucian scholarship. So, many concepts or theories which are mentioned in *Chou I* are analyzed or explained in other books and articles. Therefore, it is difficult to understand or to explain the theory of change only by the *Book of Change* without the study of these additional materials.

This study is based upon logical analysis. Even though a new theory can be analyzed empirically, in the long run establishing empirical validity is a difficult and time-consuming task. Such empirical study is left to future study; logical analysis is used here instead of the empirical study. Both individuals and groups are analyzed as actors in political change. When the acts of an individual person are in view, the causes of action, the way of action, and actors' will and mental conditions are analyzed. When a group is the object of analysis, the composition of the group, its character as a group, and relationships among group members and between it and other groups are examined.

This first chapter briefly mentions the goal, the scope, and the method of the study. In the second chapter, the concept of political change is defined and existing theories of political change are introduced—especially dynamic theories. The author explains and distinguishes among three types while pointing out their character similarities. In the third chapter, the theory of change is analyzed and defined, the general theory of change is introduced and examined in principle, and the author introduces some value claims of the *Chou I*. Among the many value claims in the *Book of Change*, this author treats only those that are connected to change theory. In the fourth chapter, the author attempts to apply the theories of change that were summarized in chapter 3 to political change. Public and the private concepts of change theory are substituted for Yin and Yang. After this substitution, the author examines the similarity between the Yin and Yang to the co-relationship of public and private interests, which are at the core of politics. At the end of that chapter, the author compares the theory of political change according to the *Chou I* to the existing theories of the political change and attempts to identify new theories of political change. The fifth chapter proposes the most favorable model of political change and examines its practicability in the real world. Chapter 6 concludes and summarizes the author's findings.

Note

1. James A. Bill & Robert L. Hardgrave Jr. COMPARATIVE POLITICS, Columbus Ohio; Charles E. Merrill Publishing Co. 1973, Chapter 2. p. 43, p. 84. Author arranged the concept of the political development and summarized the research patterns.

Chapter 2

Theories of Political Change

Definition of Political Change

The phrase *political change* combines two ideas: *politics* and *change*. The Chinese definition of politics (政治) is right governance, while the western view is the authoritative allocation of social values.[1] Change involves a transformation, an alteration, or a modification. The concept of change has two meanings. One is spontaneous morphological change from one shape to another. The other is physical change due to the intentional application of power. Change in this study includes both meanings of change: morphological—spontaneous; and intentional—physical.

Political change means change of the form of governance or change in authoritative allocation of social values. This study uses the western definition, one much wider than the Chinese.

The concept of political change is itself very wide, including spontaneous morphological change in the political structure of government, the emergence of political parties, and the formation of interest groups. It also includes constitutional, legislative, regulatory, and tax changes, as well as modification of national goals, of value claims, and of the function of governmental structures. It involves replacement of public officers, modification of the distribution of political power, and of the rules of competition for election to public office. Furthermore, the study of political change examines its causes such as changes in society, of political culture, of ideology, and of the institutional environment.

Political change was studied in ancient Greece. Aristotle analyzed causes and characteristics of revolution and constructed models of change in political systems.[2]

During the 19th century, studies of political change focused on the political system. Scholars would trace changes from absolute monarchy to constitutional monarchy through the revolutionary process of citizen revolt. Recently political scientists expanded their research method by applying scientific analysis. Developmental theory based upon evolutionism was developed in which political structure was seen as developing into parliamentary democracy through the evolutionary process. Developmental theory based upon the philosophy of dialectical materialism was also proposed, in which both causes and processes of revolution were studied. The most recent trend of study is based on developmentalism through differentiation and specialization in political structure. Thus causes, processes, and theories of change are all examined together with changes in the political culture that are at the core of the process.

There are many causes of political change. Among them are such human factors such as desire for personal honor, fear of failure and dishonor, a rebellious spirit against governing structures, and suspicion of electoral conspiracy. Political change is often prompted by environmental and demographic variations, as well as by changes in resource availability. Other factors include changes in aspects of popular culture such as political consciousness, emerging ideology, and intensifying attitudes, as well as in accelerated communication and transportation. Levels of education and alterations in the international environment are additional factors. Moreover, conflicts within society such as those between social classes, rich and poor, good and evil, traditional values and modern values, all evoke political change.

Like all other change, political change involves the dynamics of power. Power, which can scarcely act in a vacuum in the course of altering events, typically evokes some kind of contrary, opposing power. At such a moment, both forces interact, pushing and pulling in ways which produce results that vary in velocity, direction, and degree. Therefore, the study of political change should embrace assessment of the dynamics of power—its origin, volume, direction, and process.

Since the subject of political change is very broad and very complex, this study concentrates on those theories of dynamic action that seek to understand forces which engender change.

The Principle of Change in Modernization Theory

Organizing theories of political change according to a single classification tool is very difficult because political change involves the entire political processes. Since modern social scientists tend to study the subject by using similar tools, it is very difficult to distinguish particular schools of thought and to classify them accurately according to their unique characteristics. Because of this, the author has postponed such final classification, and has instead, for convenience sake, introduced three theories of political change even though some of the specific positions of various scholars overlap.

The modernization theory of political change emphasizes change caused by alteration in the social environment. In this theory, social change is an independent variable and political change a dependent variable. According to modernization theory, human society evolves and specializes gradually but with the velocity of development increasing due to developments in science and technology. When a society develops quickly and the political structure does not function adequately, political crisis, with attendant political change, follows. At such a time, if the political structure does not adjust itself to the new environment, it breaks down.

In order to explain political decay, Samuel P. Huntington used modernization theory.[3] In his view, urbanization creates popular political leaders who are difficult to control. At the same time, higher education and living standards achieved by the elites produce frustration for people left behind. Modernization of transportation systems increases mobility of population in a stratified society, leading to their more vigorous political participation and a resultant fierce conflict between conservatives and reformists. He describes this phenomenon with these simple equations:

1. $\dfrac{\text{Social mobilization}}{\text{Economic development}} = \text{Social frustration}$

2. $\dfrac{\text{Social frustration}}{\text{Mobility opportunities}} = \text{Political participation}$

3. $\dfrac{\text{Political participation}}{\text{Political institutionalization}} = \text{Political instability}$

According to this explanation, modernization of the economy and of society without necessary improvement in the political arena will increase social frustration, which in turn accelerates political participation. Then, if political structures have not kept pace, political instability follows and military intervention or a *coup d'etat* may occur. When a viable political party system does not develop, political structures fail to respond to people's demands with modified public policies. Ensuing political decay and dictatorship may then, themselves, cause even further political change.

When political participation increases, political institutionalization should increase. Institutionalization is itself a kind of political change, and the collapse of a political system due to inadequate institutionalization is another. Huntington describes the process of political collapse as a corruption of oligarchy leading to group uprisings, which, in turn, produce tension between the oligarchy and the masses. This eruption presents itself as civil strife. In explanation he offers a theory of political degeneration. ". . . [The] concept of a 'corrupt society' however, is a more familiar one in political theory. Typically it refers to a society which lacks law, authority, cohesion, discipline, and consensus, where private interests dominate public ones; in short, political institutions are weak and social forces strong. Plato's degenerate state is dominated by various forms of appetite: by forces, wealth, numbers and charisma." Finally, either personalized dictatorship or a rough democracy may appear in a corrupt society.[4]

Therefore, when political participation is expanding rapidly, a political system can be preserved by prompt institutionalization of the political structure or by control (limitation) of political participation. He insists that preservation of the political system is one of most important purposes of politics. On the other hand he is a conflict theorist, too, because he insists that political degeneration is a necessary condition for political development and that rapid modernization exacts the price of political degeneration.[5]

C.E. Black also sees causes of political change in modernization. In *Dynamics of Modernization*, he analyzes widespread changes which come from modernization in particular. According to him, modernization brings an explosive increase in knowledge; such intellectual change, in turn, brings about economic, psychological, and social change. In such a moment, new elites who have a modern outlook arise and challenge conservative elites, prompting political change. When the elites insist on a new mode of life, conservative forces either accommodate them, reject them, or attempt to make basic reforms in the political system. All modernizing societies face 1) the challenge of modernity, leading to 2) consolidation of the modernizing leadership, producing 3) economic and social transformation, with 4) attendant integration of society. There are intense power struggles between conservatives and reformists in the process. As a result of power struggles, either conservatives maintain their system or reformists achieve political reform, thus accomplishing political modernization.[6]

Karl Deutsch, S.N. Eisenstadt, and Lucian Pye insisted that political change is caused by increasing political participation and demands for greater equality in a modernizing society. According to Deutsch, social mobility demands political participation and improvement of living standards, and those demands compel governmental capacity to improve. With these increased demands comes political change.[7] Eisenstadt argues, "The central problem of political development is the ability of a political system to adapt itself to changing demands, 'to absorb them in terms of policy making' and to assure its own continuity in the face of continuous changes in political demands—the crucial test of such sustained political development."[8]

James S. Coleman and Lucian Pye understood the development syndrome as conflict caused by increasing demand for political participation.[9] Pye defined the developmental syndrome which typically arises during modernization as a crisis springing from conflict among participation, capacity, and specialization. He identifies six types of crisis.[10]

1) *Identity crisis*—Individuals feel their personal identities in part defined by their attachment to that community. Loss of such identity creates identity crisis.
2) *Legitimacy crisis*—Lack of agreement as to the legitimate nature of authority and responsibility of government.
3) *Participation crisis*—Emergence of interest groups and political parties increases demands. This expanding participation creates serious strains on existing institutions.
4) *Penetration crisis*—Political infrastructure of formal institutions links rulers and the ruled. Lack of institutionalization creates penetration crisis.

5) *Integration crisis*—Lack of connection and interaction among political groups within the political structure creates integration crisis.
6) *Distribution crisis*—A political system's inability to meet increasing demands creates distribution crisis focused on 'who gets what.'

Political development (or modernization) requires expansion of political capacity to solve problems. For this to happen, the political system must institutionalize and differentiate. Through specialization and differentiation, political systems can address conflicting demands and solve problems by creating integration. When the demand for equality increases, a political system also should increase its capabilities by creating new types of participation and distribution. In these ways political systems can solve legitimacy and integration crises. These things are causes of political change and processes by which it is brought about. Political change that is caused by increasing participation and demands for equality can also be a kind of conflict theory in which the origins of change are the same conflicts that lead to environmental change.

Dankwart A. Rustow identified environmental discontent as a cause of political change. According to him, all political action prompted by discontent is either successful or unsuccessful. When it is successful, discontented groups will disappear, but if it is unsuccessful they may give up their original political aims and challenge again, this time aiming for a more achievable goal.[11]

Similarly, theorists who seek causes of political change in modernization see the direction of political change as development and progression, and seek causes of change in environmental modernization and the conflicting dynamics between conservatives and reformists. They conclude that either degeneration and chaotic disorder or adaptation to environmental change may result in development.

Looking at results of the conflict and integration process, C.E. Black and Lucian Pye used the Anti-Integration process which is very similar to dialectic theory.

The Principle of Change in Conflict Theory

Conflict theories have long focused on dynamic actions such as complication, conflict, or competition. No matter whether it is creation, extinction, or change of existence, all change is accompanied by dynamic action, so the theory of change should be analyzed dynamically. Therefore, this section treats only theories that present conflict as an essential element of development and recommend action leading to conflict for rapid development.

Georg Hegel, Karl Marx, Charles Darwin, William Sumner, Adam Smith, and John Dewey all introduced traditional conflict theories; Fred Riggs, Lewis Coser, and David Apter presented typical conflict theories; but almost all contemporary scholars use dynamic theories in analysis of political change.

The Dialectic Theory of Hegel—Thesis-Antithesis-Synthesis—is a typical theory of conflict. According to him, when one theory or system becomes established, an opposite theory or system arises and they conflict with each other. When two theories or two systems (thesis and antithesis) conflict, their interaction results in a synthesis that is better or more developed and just than the previous norm. After the new norm (new thesis) is established, fresh opposition (a new antithesis) arises and creates another resultant (a new synthesis). As this process of Thesis-Antithesis-Synthesis continues, development continues. Complicating and conflicting relationships can occur between public and private, general will and special will, right and duty, passion and reason. Liberty increases gradually by bringing subjective liberty into conflict with objective liberty. Because this process is performed by the Absolute, or Spirit, development is inevitable. Hegel saw complication and conflict as factors essential to development. Therefore, even though war threatens life and property, states choose war consciously because these threats are productive, although they also result in further threat to life and property.

At this point, Hegel committed a critical error. In his analysis of traditional and modern, he concluded that European Christian society was the final goal toward which development moves. Therefore, there is no war among European states, but wars between European society and developing societies—and wars among developing societies—are inevitable and necessary for further development. According to him, as long as there is a developing society on earth, war is inevitable.[12]

Karl Marx used Hegel's dialectical developmentalism and established dialectical historicism and materialism. Marx denied Hegel's Absolute Spirit and even negated the inner motivation of human beings. He insisted on a materialism that motivates all human beings since they are totally controlled by external factors. He held that the class struggle which arises from economic factors brings development to society. Conflict between lord and slave, employer and employee, bourgeoisie and proletariat, all inevitably invite the evolutionary development of history, and eventuate in a communist society—the ideal society without any private property.

Marx's theory of actions that produce change is not Hegel's process of Thesis-Antithesis-Synthesis, but rather a continuous negation process in which an opposing power arises to negate any existing norm, and establishes a new norm. Then a subsequent opposing power arises to negate that norm. Ideal society is finally achieved by this process. Because he believed the final, inevitable end of this process to be a good and right society, he advocated acceleration of the conflicts which fuel it. Thus he fell into self-contradiction. In other words, he calls for conflict as the means to a conflictless end.[13]

Conflict theorists uniformly present such conflicting actions as competition, opposition, and struggle as essential factors for developmental change. Ali A. Mazrui and Lewis A. Coser analyzed several materials and emphasized conflict theory. Mazrui introduced conflict theory in his thesis "From Social Darwinism to Current Theories of Modernization."[14]

Evolutionism as set forth by Charles Darwin saw competition as the power driving development. In *Origin of Species*, he insisted that the general law of evolution of living things is breeding and transformation and that the direction of such change is due to their adaptation to their environment and its necessities. Thus, the stronger survive and the weaker perish. Furthermore, he insisted that human virtue and morality develop similarly. The conflict between highly moral and less moral behavior is an incentive for humans to follow higher morality, and to choose virtue over vice. Though the process of development is slow or may pause because of hindrances, just like human development, morality also develops by laws of nature. In other words, according to Darwin the pattern of struggle for existence is justified by the developmental direction of human society, and the origin of development is competition, a rule of nature that the stronger who adapt well to the environment will prevail over the weaker who do not.[15]

Ali A. Mazrui treated liberal economic theory as a kind of Darwinism. He agreed with William G. Sumner that society was a contest in which each individual struggled for his own good and had to encroach upon some interests of others in order to realize his own interest. Survival was for the imaginative, the ruthless, the industrious, the frugal. The indolent and extravagant lost out in the struggle, incapable as they were of adapting to the realities of life. They were therefore eliminated by a process of "social selection." Sumner insisted that a society is one of either " . . . liberty, inequality, and survival of the fittest [or] not-liberty, equality, and survival of the unfittest."[16]

He also cited the free market theory of Adam Smith in which

> . . . each individual pursuing his own interest might indeed gain at the expense of another, but that somehow an 'invisible hand' guided this process of intensive individualistic competition toward a better capability of the species as a whole. Man's innate tendency to 'truck, barter, and trade,' when given natural freedom to express itself free of encumbrances from the state, would automatically develop in the direction of economic well-being of the society as a whole.[17]

He sees John Dewey's theory of consciousness and thought as arising in the wake of obstacles to the interaction of groups: "Conflict is the gadfly of thought. It stirs us to observation and memory. It instigates to invention. It shocks us out of sheep-like passivity, and sets us at noting and contriving. . . . Conflict is a *sine qua non* of reflection and ingenuity."[18] So Sumner, Smith, and Dewey all agree that development comes from free competition and the struggle for existence.

Ali A. Mazrui used not only competition, but also struggle as engines of development. Citing Huntington's analysis, he explained creative conflict as ". . . almost anything that happens in 'developing' countries—coups, ethnic struggles, revolutionary war—[that] becomes part of the process of development, however contradictory or retrogressive this may appear on the surface."[19] He also cited David Apter and Eisenstadt who explained that conflict between traditionalism and modernism is a precondition of development, and that social conflict is a source of modernization.[20]

In the article "Social Conflict and the Theory of Social Change," Lewis A. Coser introduced theories of George Sorel, Sidney Sufrin, Thorstein Veblem, and Karl Marx.[21] In his book, *Reflections on Violence*, Sorel insisted that just as

> . . . antagonistic classes influence each other in a partially and indirect but decisive manner. . . conflict (violence) prevents ossification of the social system by exerting pressure for innovation and creativity. . . The gradual disappearance of class conflict might well lead to the decadence of European culture. A social system, he felt, was in need of conflict if

only to renew its energies and revitalize its creative forces.... Conflict within and between groups in a society can prevent accommodations and habitual relations from progressively impoverishing creativity. The clash of values and interests, the tension between what is and what some groups feel ought to be, the conflict between vested interests and new strata and groups demanding their share of power, wealth and status, have been productive of vitality.[22]

Sidney C. Sufrin and conservative British economists have pointed out that union pressure goads management into technical improvement and increased capital investment.[23] Melville Dalton insisted that conflict among departments within a state motivate development of the state because "[C]onflict within and between bureaucratic structures provides means for avoiding ossification and ritualism which threatened their form of organization."[24]

Through the concept of "vested interest," Thorstein Veblem portrayed conflicts between "haves" and "have nots" as similar to Karl Marx's theory of class struggle.

"Any social system implies an allocation of power, as well as wealth and status position among individual actors and component subgroups. As has been pointed out, there is never complete concordance between what individuals and groups within a system consider their just due and the system of allocation. Conflict ensues in the efforts of various frustrated groups and individuals to increase their share of gratification. Their demands will encounter resistance from those who previously had established a "vested interest" in a given form of distribution of honor, wealth and power. To vested interests, an attack against their position necessarily appears as an attack upon the social order. Those who derive privileges from a given system of allocation of status, wealth, and power will perceive an attack upon those prerogatives as an attack against the system itself."

The very conflicts between them are factors of change. He also analyzed the process of change.[25] According to him,

> [M]ere 'frustration' and the ensuing strains and tensions do not necessarily lead to group conflict. Individuals under stress may relieve their tension through 'acting out' in special safety valve institutions in as far as they are provided for in the social system... [S]train leads to emergence of specific new patterns of behavior of whole groups of individuals who pursue 'optimization of gratification.' By choosing what they

consider appropriate means for maximization of rewards, social change which reduces sources of their frustration may come about. This may happen in two ways: if the social system is flexible enough to adjust to conflict situations we will deal with change within the system. If, on the other hand, the social system is not able to readjust itself and allows accumulation of conflict, 'aggressive' groups, imbued with a new system of values which threatens to split the general consensus of society, and imbued with an ideology which 'objectifies' their claims, may become powerful enough to overcome the resistance of vested interests and bring about breakdown of the system and emergence of a new distribution of social values.

On the other hand, Marx defined economic class as a conflicting factor.

Economic conditions have first transformed the mass of the population into workers. The domination of capital created for this mass a common situation and common interest. This mass was thus already a class as against capital, but not for itself. It is in struggle . . .that the mass gathers together and constitutes itself as a class for itself. The interests which it defends become class interests.

As mentioned above, Mazrui and Coser emphasize that dynamic relationships such as conflict, opposition, and struggle bring social change. According to them, there is no development without conflict, and conflict is the inevitable price of development.

C.E. Black sees modernization as a result of the improvement of science and knowledge, but in explaining the changing process he uses conflict theory. According to him, "Modernization is the process by which historically evolved institutions are adapted to rapidly changing functions that reflect the unprecedented increase in man's knowledge, permitting that control over his environment that accompanied the scientific revolution." His analysis can be summarized in the following paragraph.[26]

When its knowledge grows, humanity prospers, but its beliefs and value claims change. Human life becomes more complicated and social problems increase. In such times reformists' challenges to existing leadership bring change as the conflict between them becomes intense. Construction of a new way of life inevitably is accompanied by destruction of the old. Reintegration of societies on the basis of new principles involves disintegration of traditional ones. "In a reasonably well-integrated society institutions work effectively; people are in general agreement as to ends and means, and violence and disorder are kept at a low level. But when a rapid change of environment is introduced, different elements of the society do not adapt themselves at the same rate, and disorder may become so complete that widespread violence breaks out, large numbers of people emigrate, and normal government becomes impossible. There are several types of violence between traditionalists and reformists with leadership change sometimes accomplished through the very cruel processes of civil war. In the conflict between levels of power, centralized national politics evolves in an attempt to preserve the integrity of the state. Sometimes conflict between powers seeking independence from those seeking to enforce dependence provokes an international crisis and creates a new international order."

According to conflict theorists, conflict, opposition, competition, and struggle in the process of modernization are natural human behaviors, and when reformists capture traditionalists' position and seek to exert control, the greatest crisis follows. Though there is some violence and intense struggle at that time, in the long run all these processes improve human civilization and benefit humanity.

In "The Dialectics of Developmental Conflict," Fred W. Riggs introduced conflict theories by using Lucian Pye's concepts of "Equality, Capacity, and Differentiation" and Gabriel Almond's "structural functionalism." In his book *Aspects of Political Development*, Pye described "Acute Tension" as a major characteristic of the development syndrome.[27] He defined "equality" as participation of the masses in politics; "capacity" as effective and efficient application of public policy of government giving influence to the whole society; "differentiation" as a government's letting each of its departments specialize; and "integration" a government's harmonizing several complex branches into one harmonious whole. There is "Acute Tension" in all these interrelations. Demands for equality challenge the capacity of a system, but differentiation, by emphasizing specialized skills, reduces equality. On the other hand, Almond's Structural Functional Theory defines the political system as an institutionalizing structure which solves conflicting problems. In it, conflict solving and decision making are identified as major functions of government. He called this function "Conversion" while Parsons called it "Integration."[28] Pye's "Acute Tension" means a kind of conflict, and Almond's structural functionalism also makes conflict a precondition. By using both Pye's and Almond's theories, Riggs defined conflicts among classes, races, religions, languages, individuals, tribes and conflict among departments of government as normal functions, and analyzed conflict solving as "conversion." Parsons had named it "Integration." By Riggs' postulation, elites hold more power than the masses and tend to seek and preserve more and more power. "However, some members of the masses, or of the sub-elite, appreciate the connection between power and those valued prizes generated by the system. Members of the elite tend to resist their demands." Ultimately, Riggs' analysis is similar to Thorstein Veblen's "Vested Interest."

He also used Pye's generalization of the power relationship as a typical rationalization for preserving power used by ruling elites who seek to increase capacity, while the demands of the ruled are expressed as a quest for more equality. This can be represented by a diagram showing a zero-sum relationship. It suggests that when relative equality increases, capacity decreases, and that when capacity increases, equality decreases. This relationship is applicable to the tradition-reform relationship and to the leftists-rightists relationship, and is fundamentally a dialectical one.[29]

According to Riggs, when society is more differentiated and specialized, society can increase in both equality and capacity. He also characterized a society in which specialized departments are well-coordinated

Figure 2-1
Mutual Conflict

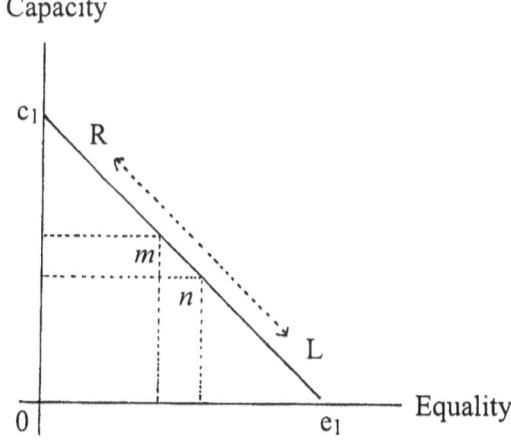

Material: Fred W. Riggs, A Dialectics of Developmental Conflicts, ibid. p. 204.

as being *synthesized* or *integrated*. When both differentiation and integration function well, he applied the term *diffraction*; but when differentiation is good but integration is not sufficient, he called this condition *prismatic*. In diffraction both equality and capacity improve resulting in development. But in a *prismatic* society—one that is well-differentiated but not well-integrated—conflicts and struggles become intense. This situation is characteristic of developing societies.[30]

Riggs saw this conflict between equality and capacity both in the transition from monarchy to republic and in the class struggle seen in modern society. He also explained the development of modern constitutional government as a result of conflict between insiders (appointed professional bureaucrats) and outsiders (officials elected by public demands). He saw increasing participation arising during the conflict between rulers and the ruled. His analysis suggests that conflicts among nations grow out of stronger states' need for security and weaker ones' demands for equality.[31]

The Principle of Change-in-Balance Theory

The *system, structural functional, group,* and *balance of power* are all *balance* theories. According to their theorists, a balanced system is able to sustain itself and maintain its stability. In an out-of-balance system, resultant conflict tends to move a system toward balance and stability. Establishment of a new balance is a kind of change, but it does not necessarily involve change of the system itself. Destruction of a system means change, and transference of equilibrium means either development or degeneration of that system, so these theories seek to explain the power of political changes.

The system theory and the structural functional theory both treat political society as one of structure or system, emphasizing concepts of "input," "output," "feedback," and "environment," with their focus on the function of a political system and the structure and function of organs within that system, as well as balance among them all. This theory was first introduced as a mechanical structure emphasizing balanced functions, but was later explained as an organic theory in which a political society can either grow or degenerate as its equilibrium either increases or decreases.

Within a given structure, if one component grows another may decline. In another structure if one component grows, the other may also grow. In the first case, the two variables are in conflict. Therefore, maintaining balance between them allows the structure to continue to function. When imbalance occurs, the structure fails to function and its breakdown provokes formation of a new structure. This view fits with Pye's theory of the interaction between equality and capacity. In the second case, there is that kind of relationship in which if one component grows or declines, the other component grows too. In the former relationship, two variables conflict with each other, so two variables must maintain balance for normal function. When one component is excessive it creates imbalance and the structure becomes dysfunctional—the structure breaks down and a new structure is formed. This kind of relationship is similar to Pye's concept of equality and capacity. In the latter case, in which both components increase proportionately, the political system can continue to function. Huntington's model of co-relationship between demand and capacity is such a relationship. In it, if demand increases without a similar increase in capacity, the political system breaks down. "Over-institutionalization is conducive to establishment of repressive order; participation far beyond institutional capacity may foster unacceptable instability and political decay."[32] When both demand and capacity increase in balance, the political system grows; when both decrease in balance it degenerates but does not completely break down. So his theory has a logic somewhat similar to organic theory.[33]

Fred W. Riggs also introduced the developmental model which is organic and in which political structure grows with the increase of both demand and capacity. When the curve changes from 1 to 3 in Figure 2-3,

Figure 2-2
Huntington's Model of Political Development

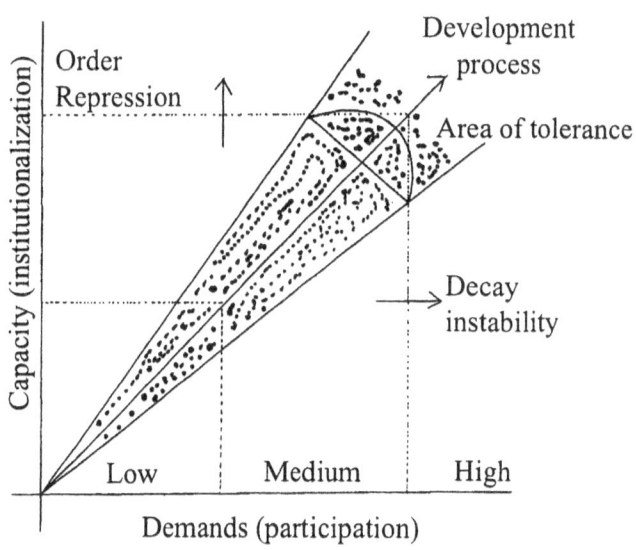

Material: Bill & Hardgrave, COMPARATIVE POLITICS, ibid. p. 80.

both equality and capacity are increasing and the zone of conflict (R-I, Acute Tension) is narrowing.

William C. Mitchell studied changing components of political structure.[34] He defined the political system as an assembly of several components which are continuously changing, but at varying rates. He analyzed

Figure 2-3
Riggs' Model of Development Differentiation and Increasing Compatibility Curves

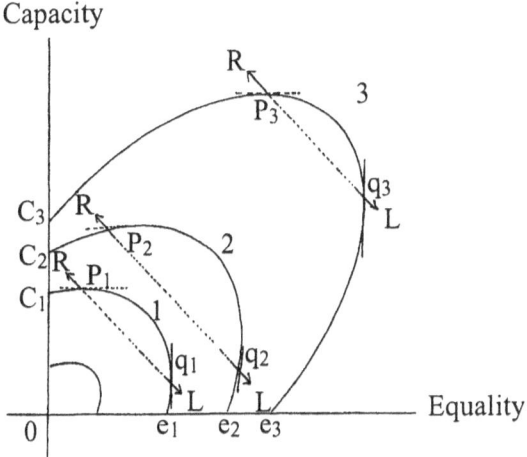

Material: Fred Riggs, A Dialectics of Developmental Conflicts, COMPARATIVE POLITICAL STUDIES 1, July, 1968. pp. 197-226.

the influence of each component's change upon the other components and upon the system as a whole. He focused especially on 1) major components of political structure, 2) the velocity of change of components, and 3) relationships among components. Mitchell addressed multiple components of political structure: political culture such as value claims, attitudes, and beliefs; formal institutions of political structure such as political parties, parliaments, and bureaucracies; formal and informal institutions of society; political elites who have influence in society; and deliberate policies of government.

Balance theorists consider imbalance to be a cause of change. Manfred Halpern held that imbalance among societies or imbalance among components of society causes change. Even the will and ability to normalize imbalance cause change.[35]

In analyzing participation and institutionalization, Huntington also considered imbalance as a driving force in change. An imbalance between participation and institutionalization provides an incentive to institutionalize. If unchecked, imbalance can motivate whole-system change—even revolution.[36]

Organic theory is a typical way of explaining transference of the balance point, or equilibrium. Organic theory adopted a living organism as a representative of human society. Just as a live organism bears, grows, and dies, a society also bears, grows, and dies. Just as a live organism grows when a body functions well in a balanced condition, degenerates when a body functions weakly, and dies when a body does not function at all, so does society grow when it functions well in a balanced condition, degenerate when it functions weakly, and breaks down when paralyzed. This amounts to a kind of *living system* theory.

Balance theorists place more emphasis on stability than on change. Huntington treats change as abnormal and unnatural, stability and equilibrium as normal and natural.

"In its pure form, the theory conceives of equilibrium as a state of rest. In all forms it presupposes tendencies toward restoration of an original condition or a theoretically defined condition of equilibrium." . . . "In effect, change is viewed as an extraneous abnormality. It is held to be the result of strain or tension, which gives rise to compensating movements that tend to reduce strain or tension and thus restore the original state. Change is 'unnatural;' stability or rest is 'natural.'"[37]

Huntington thought change to be abnormal and unnatural, but stability and equilibrium, normal and natural. To him, all conflicts and struggles that arise within social structures, such as those for equality with an opposing elite, class struggles, and struggles for existence, are reconstructive and functional actions tending to create a new equilibrium. Unlike a living organism, the creation and death of a society are uncertain, and any period of society is part of a line of continuous development from past to future. In this process, if imbalance among components occurs, society changes in order to create a new balance. He compared this phenomenon to an earthquake. According to natural scientists, an earthquake is an abnormal, but nevertheless necessary, means for maintaining balance for the earth. The stronger or more frequent the quakes, the greater the consequent changes in the surface of the earth.[38]

Conflict theorists hold imbalance, inequality, and discontinuity to be as important as balance, equality, and continuity. They consider violent events and struggles as basic to the process of political-social relationships. In contrast, balance theorists consider conflict, tension, competition, and violence as abnormal happenings or derailments. According to them, these abnormal phenomena are consciously allowable only on condition that the political system be sustained and abnormality controlled. For them, stability is itself a goal of social science; revolutionary changes are treated as abnormal phenomena even for revolutionists, as well as for the people who suffer from revolution. Generally, their view is that development toward modernity is most likely to happen within a stable political system.

Both the group theory and the balance-of-power theory emphasize the importance of stability and balance. Group theory as proposed by David B. Truman and Arthur F. Bently has been further expanded by many scholars. According to it, a political system is a complex network of interrelated groups. The relationships among groups can be either competitive and conflictual or cooperative. Interaction among groups creates either tension or cooperation, and instances of conflict or cooperation become important elements in societal development. The value of group theory lies in the fact that it allows analysis of the processes of gathering and accumulation of interests and values, as well as analysis of the decision-making process. Group analysts treat the process of modernization as one of formalization, complication, differentiation, specialization, and integration.[39]

The group approach places heavy emphasis upon such concepts as equilibrium and balance. "When the equilibrium is threatened, the process is described as disturbance or disruption within group perspective, the important patterns and functions are integrative in nature." Group theorists frequently employ such concepts as consensus, cohesion, coalition, coalescence, combination, alliance, agreement, bargaining, reciprocation, negotiation, uniformity, and conformity. Disintegration, division, and disagreement are treated as aberrant patterns. Group analysis is less effective in its analysis of change, especially of its more extreme forms.

Group scholars view the socio-political system as a huge, fluctuating, but stabilizing, web of groups. Though conflict and competition are sometimes evident, they are seen to serve the continuity and preservation of the system. "The system is taken as a given, and its maintenance is explained in terms of checks and balances within and among groups. Countervailing pressures and equilibrating tensions may in the short run account for modifications in power relations, but in the long run, they always contribute to system stability." Group theory, although somewhat like conflict theory, more nearly resembles balance theory with its emphasis on stability and equilibrium.

The balance-of-power theory was introduced by Hans J. Morganthau as a theory of international relationships; it has characteristics similar to both system theory and group theory. His view is based on the logic of Charles Darwin's *struggle for existence* (in which suitable beings survive). This theory accepts competition for power among nations and is typically realistic. According to it, peace can exist only during times of a balance of power among nations. When the balance of power shifts requiring a new balance, struggle or war among nations can arise. Therefore, in order to sustain peace a balance of power should be maintained through increase or decrease of military forces.[40]

Western theories of political change and dynamic principles were introduced, as mentioned above. Modernization is addressed both by evolutionary and developmental theories. Although they explain the process of modernization and societal development very well, they have difficulty in explaining retrogression and they fail to explain dysfunction in or degeneration of society. In addition, they are vague about the end toward which development moves.

Conflict theorists explain the causes, processes, and dynamics of change fairly well. They hold that competition and conflict motivate development. But because they treat competition and conflict as essential conditions for development, they foster the very disorder and disturbance that most human beings hate. They also neglect the value of integration. Moreover, they presume that the goal toward which a society moves will be the optimum society. Then they advocate struggle and active conflict to expedite reaching this goal.

Balance theories explain power relations within political structures and functions of political systems quite well, but because they emphasize system preservation it is difficult for such theories to account for system-wide change and they do not even address revolutionary change.

As can be seen in the descriptions given in this chapter, all theories of political change have strong points and weak points, as they offer their views of specific aspects of political change.

Notes

1. David Easton, THE POLITICAL SYSTEM, New York: Alfred A. Knopf.1953, p. 128.
2. Kim, Hack June, 金學俊, 現代政治過程論, 서울: 法文社. 1978, p. 387, p. 404.
3. Huntington wrote in many of writings. Samuel P. Huntington, "Political Development and Political Decay," WORLD POLITICS 17, April, 1965, p. 386-430, "The Change to Change, Modernization, Development, and Politics," COMPARATIVE POLITICS 3, April, 1971, p. 314, THE POLITICAL ORDER IN CHANGING SOCIETIES, p. 55.
4. Samuel P. Huntington, "Political Development and Political Decay", ibid, p. 416, Huntington cited the contents of the book, THE REPUBLIC, THE LORD OF THE FLIES, A HISTORY OF POLITICAL THOUGHT.
5. Samuel P. Huntington, "Political Development and Political Decay," ivid, p. 415, Bill & Harhgrave, COMPARATIVE POLITICS, Ohio: Chares E. Merril Publishing Co. 1973, p. 77.
6. C.E. Black, THE DYNAMICS OF MODERNIZATION, New York, Harper & Row Publishers Co. 1966.
7. Karl Deutsch, "Social Mobilization and Political Development," AMERICAN POLITICAL SCIENCE REVIEW 55, Sept. 1961, p. 494, Adopted by Bill & Hardgrave, COMPARATIVE POLITICS, p. 76.
8. S.N/Eisenstadt, "Initial Institutional Patterns of Political Mobilization," CIVILIZATION 12. Adopted by Bill & Hardgrave, COMPARATIVE POLITICS, ibid, p. 74.
9. James S. Coleman, "The Development Syndrome: Differentiation Equality Capacity" in SSRC Committee, CRISES AND SEQUENCES, p. 7. Adopted by Bill & Hardgrave, ibid, p. 69.
10. Lucian Pye, ASPECTS OF POLITICAL DEVELOPMENT, Boston; Little Brown, 1966. p. 65, SSRC Committee, CRISIS AND SEQUENCES, pp. 101-282, Bill and Hardgrave, ibid. p. 70.
11. Dankwart A. Rustow, "Change as the Theme of Political Science," pp. 6-8, and CHANGE IN COMMUNIST SYSTEM, Stanford, 1970. Pp. 343-358. Adopted by Samuel P. Huntington, "The Change to Change," ibid. p. 320.
12. Leo Straus & Joseph Cropsey, HISTORY OF POLITICAL PHILOSOPHY, Chicago: The University of Chicago Press, 1981, p. 686, p. 712. They summarized the books, THE PHILOSOPHY OF RIGHT, LECTURES ON HE PHILOSOPHY OF HISTORY, PHENOMENOLOGY OF MIND.
13. Leo Straus & Joseph Cropsey, HISTORY OF POLITICAL PHILOSOPHY, ibid, p. 755, p. 781. They summarized THE COMMUNIST MANIFESTO, THE GERMAN IDEOLOGY.

14. Ali A. Mazrui, "From Social Darwinism to Current Theories of Modernization; A Traditional Analysis," WORLD POLITICS 21, Oct. 1968. pp. 69-83.
15. Ali A. Mazrui, ibid. p. 80.
16. Richard Hofstadter, SOCIAL DARWINISM IN AMERICAN THOUGHT 1860-1915,. Philadelphia: 1944, Adopted by Ali A. Mazrui, ibid, p. 80.
17. Ali A. Mazrui, ibid. p. 80
18. Lewis A. Coser, "Social Conflict and the Theory of Social Change," BRITISH JOURNAL OF SOCIOLOGY 8, Sept. 1957, pp. 197-207. He cited John Dewey, HUMAN NATURE AND CONDUCT, The Modern Library, 1930. p. 300.
19. Ali A. Mazrui, ibid. p. 81
20. Ali A. Mazrui, ibid. p. 82. He cited Eisenstadt, MODERNIZATKION, and David Apter, THE POLITICS OF MODERNIZATION, Chicago: 1965.
21. Lewis A. Coser, ibid. pp. 197-207.
22. George Sorel, REFLECTION ON VIOLENCE, Chapter 2, Part 2, Adopted by Lewis A. Coser. Ibid. p. 197-198.
23. Will Herbert, "When Social Scientists View Labor," COMMUNITY, Dec. 1951, pp. 5900-596, Seymour Melman, DYNAMIC FUTURE IN INDUSTRIAL PRODUCTIVITY, Oxford: Black Well, 1956, Adopted by Lewis A. Coser, Ibid. p. 198.
24. Melville Dalton, "Conflict between Staff and Line managerial Officers," AM.SIC.R.15, 1950. pp. 342-351. Adopted by Lewis A. Coser, ibid, p. 200.
25. Thorstein Veblem, THE VESTED INTEREST AND THE STATE OF THE INDUSTRIAL ART, N.Y.; 1919, Max Lerner, "Vested interests" ENCYCLOPAEDIA OF THE SOCIAL SCIENCE, 15. p. 240, Quoted by Lewis A. Coser, ibid. p. 203-204.
26. C.E. Black, THE DYNAMICS OF MODERNIZATION, New York: Harper & Row Publisher, 1967.
27. Lucian W. Pye, ASPECTS OF POLITICAL DEVELOPMENT, Boston: Little Brown, 1966. pp. 45-48. Quoted by Fred W. Riggs, "The Dialectics of Developmental Conflicts," COMPARATIVE POLITICAL STUDIES I, July, 1968, pp. 197-226.
28. Gabriel Almond and Bingham Powell, Jr. COMPARATIVE POLITICS; A DEVELOPMENTAL APPROACH, Boston: Little Brown, 1966, p. 35. Quoted by Fred W. Riggs, ibid. p. 199.
29. Fred W. Riggs. Ibid. pp. 203-204.
30. Fred W. Riggs, ibid. p. 207.
31. Fred W. Riggs, ibid. p. 210-224.
32. Bill & Hardgrave, COMPARATIVE POLITICS, Columbus, Bell & Howell Co. 1973. p. 80.
33. Samuel P. Huntington, POLITICAL ORDER IN CHANGING SOCIETY, ibid. p. 55.

34. William C. Mitchell, THE AMERICAN POLITY, New York: 1962. p. 369, Cited by Huntington, "The Change to Change," ibid. p. 315.
35. Manfred Halpern, "The Rate and Costs of Political Development," ANNALS 358, March, 1965. p. 22, Cited by Bill & Hardgrave Jr. COMPARATIVE POLITICS, ibid. p. 75.
36. Bill & Hardgrave, COMPARATIVE POLITICS, ibid. pp. 80.
37. Samuel P. Huntington, "The Change To Change," ibid. p. 308.
38. Walderman Kaemfert, "Science in Review," NEW YORK TIMES, July/27/1952. Cited by Lewis A. Coser, ibid. p. 201.
39. Bill & Hardgrave, COMPARATIVE POLITICS, ibid. p. 117-141. They arranged all the theories of group analysis up to the date of this chapter.
40. Hans J. Morgenthau, POLITICS AMONG NATIONS, New York: Alfred A. Knopf Inc. 1978.

Chapter 3

The Theory of Change (易理)

Definition of Chou I (周易)

The Chinese letter (易) means a change in variation, while I Hsüch (易學) is the science of change. Specifically, I Hsüch means the science of change of the Chou dynasty, so-called Chou I (周易); it does not encompass all sciences of change. I Hsüch is philosophical because it is based on metaphysical principles. In the analysis of creation and the change of all things and the universe, mathematical principles and scientific studies were used so it could be treated as a natural science—like physics or astronomy. It also exhibits some ethical characteristics because it connects the principle of change to natural law and to humanity, and because it claims some moral principles. Additionally, if one understands the principle of change thoroughly, future change can be predicted, so it is also used as an art of divination. Chou I attempted to connect the theories of the origination and the death of all things and affairs and the theory of the process of the creation of the universe to the human principle of good or bad luck and the fairness or partiality.

Chou I presumes the quantity and the shape, and induces the theory of change from two basic elements, the Yin and Yang (anion and cation), so it seems to be a theory of materialism. But because it admits unchangeable principles and emphasizes the moral principle of medium and the principle of encouragement—encouraging Yang and discouraging Yin—it is not a theory of materialism; in general, it is called a theory of evaporation. (氣化論).

Chou I contains three meanings of change: the theory of simple change (簡易); the theory of change (變易); and the theory of no change (不易). The theory of simple change shows the simplified shapes and models of the items and phenomena of nature. The theory of change means that no affairs nor things are unchangeable and that nature and human destiny are changing continuously. The theory of no change means there exists unchangeable principles—even in the changing condition, there are unchangeable orders in nature and unchangeable principles of change.

The author of *Chou I* is not known. In the book *Chou Li* (周禮), there is a record of three books of change about the great divination (太卜三易). First is *The Continuous Mountains* (連山), second is *The Return to Hide* (歸藏), and third is *Chou I* (周易). In the book, *Praise of Change* (易贊), of the post Han dynasty, Cheng Hsuan (鄭玄) wrote, "The continuous mountains means continuously connected mountains, because the Kên hexagram was a top hexagram during the Hsia dynasty (夏) they called this book *The Continuous Mountains*; the Return to Hide means going back and hiding, so this book was called *The Return to Hide*. Chou I means the change book of the Chou Dynasty. According to this book, natural phenomena and human destiny are not fixed but are changing continuously, so it was called *The Book of Change, Chou I* (周易) or *I Ching* (易經)." Therefore, it was known that there were two books of change, *The Continuous Mountains* and *The Return to Hide*, before *Chou I*. But these two books are not transmitted and studied.[1]

Chou I is based on Ho Tu (河圖) and Lo Shu (洛書); their origins are not clear. In general, the legend of Ho Tu, Fui Shih (伏羲氏) followed the pattern of the back style of a dragon horse who came out of the Yellow River and drew the eight trigrams (八卦). In the legend of Lo Shu, when Hsia Yü Shih (夏禹氏) embanked the Lo river (洛水) he found the numerals on the back of the mysterious tortoise which came out of the river and granted Chiu Chou (九疇).[2]

The writer of the eight trigrams and 64 hexagrams is not certain, but it is known that Fui Shih drew eight trigrams and King Wen (文王) reached the great accomplishment of developing change theory. King Wen wrote the explanations of the hexagrams (卦辭) and his son, Chou Kung (周公), wrote the additional explanations of each line of the hexagrams (爻辭). Also, it is known that Confucius wrote ten wings of Chou I (十翼) (or ten wings of Confucius). They are: Wen Yen (文言) (especially Wen Yen Chuan of Chien Kua (乾卦文言傳) and Wen Yen Chuan of Kun Kua (坤卦文言傳); Tuan Tzu (彖辭); two images, Large Image (大象) and Little Image (小象); two great treatises, Upper Chi Tzu Chuan (繫辭上傳) and Lower Chi Tzu Chuan (繫辭下傳); Shuo Kua Chuan (說卦傳); Hsü Kua Chuan (序卦傳); and Tsa Kua Chuan (雜卦傳).

The study of change began before the Yin dynasty and that study increased during the Chou dynasty. When Confucianism became popular after Confucius, *Chou I* became one of the nine basic books of Confucianism (四書五經) and all the students of the Confucian school studied it. Chu Hsi (朱熹) of China and Toegae (退溪) of Korea also had studied *Chou I* in-depth. Chu Hsi left the book *I Hsüch Chi Meng* (易學啟蒙) after he studied it, and Toegae left the book *Chi Meng Chuan I* (啟蒙傳疑) at the end of his studies. In the latter, Toegae collected all the questionable points and left them to future wise men to elucidate.

The Kua Tzu (卦辭), the Hsiao Tzu (爻辭), and the ten wings of Confucius compose *Chou I*. The Kua Tzu explains the 64 hexagrams. Each hexagram is constructed with an upper trigram and a lower trigram. The Kua Tzu connects these trigrams to the characters of the eight trigrams—the heaven (天), the earth (地), water (水), fire (火), thunder (雷), the wind (風), the mountain (山), and the pond (澤)—and explains the characteristics of the hexagrams and their characters of change.

The Hsiao Tzu explains the good or ill luck of each line in the hexagrams according to its characteristics—Yin or Yang, position, number, etc. The Tuan Tzu explains the Kua Tzu, or hexagrams, according to the position of medium and justice (中正), and affirms the end of things and affairs. The Hsiang Tzu explains gains and losses according to its shape and lines. The Large Image explains the shape of the hexagram and the Small Image explains the shape and the situation of each line of the hexagram.

The Chi Tzu Chuan connects the hexagram to the line. It makes general remarks concerning the entire *Chou I* and theorizes principles of change from the relationships among the heaven, the earth, and human beings; from the relationship between Yin and Yang and between sturdiness and weakness. It connects the natural order to human life and expresses great admiration of *Chou I*.

The Wen Yen explains only two hexagrams—the Chien and the Kun—through the concepts of origin, good will, interest, righteousness (元亨利貞), submission (柔順), and medium and justice (中正).

Shuo Kua Chuan (說卦傳) explains the eight pure hexagrams (乾、坤、坎、離、兌、巽、震、艮) according to the direction and the comparison of things, and explains the establishment of the hexagram and the principle of divination. Hsü Kua Chuan (序卦傳) establishes the order of the 64 hexagrams according to the natural order and principles of human affairs. Tsa Kua Chuan (雜卦傳) explains the significance of each hexagram and compares the shape according to the king's position (second line of the upper trigram) and subject's position (second line of the lower trigram).

In order to explain the principle of change, an explanation of two other items is required. These are the theory of the origin of all things, Tai Chi Shuo (太極說), and a numeric description of the principle of the creation of all things, Ho Tu and Lo Shu.

The function and the usage of the theory of change is decided by the contents of the theories. Even though the theory of the creation of the universe and the atomic theory of the Yin-Yang are impossible to verify empirically, the study of the theory of change has some significance. First of all, the science of change defines the movement of the earth and celestial bodies as a cause of change in all things and explains the changes of nature upon the movement of a celestial sphere. As a result, it finds the changing process to be dependent on the day, month, season, and year, and attempts to understand the relationship between humans and their environment, so suggesting the proper way of living. When human behavior coincides with the laws of nature, it is expressed as a union of heaven and human (天人合一). Any behavior which coincides with the laws of nature is called a rational action and any behavior which goes against the laws of nature is called an irrational action. This type of assertion is sometimes criticized as being fatalistic because it ties the human future to nature and implies a stagnated condition, but the theory recognizes the human ability of self-development and hints that humans can change their own future within a given environment. Therefore, the theory of change recognizes the independence and the sincerity of human beings. But if man behaves against the laws of nature he will suffer defeat; if man tries to harmonize to the laws of nature he may be successful. Thus, the theory of change is a kind of naturalism.

Second, because the theory of change is a science used to analyze the principles of change and the state of timely affairs, it is contributory to the studies of the principle of change, the process of change, and the dynamic principle of change of timely affairs. Because the theory of change treats the basic principle of change, it can be applicable to all affairs; it treats not only natural science, but also social science.

Third, knowing the principles of change makes prediction of the future possible. If one finds the principle of change and if it is an unchangeable principle, one can predict the future exactly. For example, if one knows the change of nature according to the change of season, one can know the happenings of next spring. Similarly, one can predict the political change of the next election season if one knows the political changes according to the election cycle.

Fourth, the theory of change is known to have predictability abilities beyond human ability. Because this function is beyond human ability, it is impossible to verify by scientific methods but many people have selected this book as a divination book and have used it for that purpose. *Chou I* adopted the trigonometric function of the heaven, the earth, and the human being, and distinguished between Yin and Yang based on the numbers of Ho Tu and Lo Shu, then developed a hexagram from them. The resulting hexagram is one of the aforementioned 64 hexagrams. *Chou I* relates the state of the condition of a particular man in a particular time to one of the 64 hexagrams, explains the given situation, and insists the logical responsibility of that explanation—but it is impossible to verify scientifically.

Finally, the theory of change seems to contribute significantly to the study of social change. These days, social scientists and political scientists are very much interested in developmental changes. They have studied the goals of change, the processes of change, and the dynamics of change, and many of them chose dialectical conflict, opposition, and integration as a changing principle. *Chou I* may correct the weaker points of dialectical theories and may reinforce the conflict theories.

But the *Chou I* also has a few problems. The theories of Tai Chi, Ho Tu, and Lo Shu, which form the basis of Chou I theory, are metaphysical theories. As such, they are impossible to verify. The principles of human morality which were deduced from the laws of nature also lack the logical connection between the laws of nature and a mental state of human beings. There have been a few attempts to try to connect the human mind to the heavenly mind or to the laws of nature: The theory of the mind passing through the passion and rationality of Cheng, Fu Hsin (程復心, 心統性情論); the theory of unanimity of the heaven and human minds of Kuen, Yang Chon (天人心合一論, 權陽村); the theory of heaven's order (天命論); the theory of the mind passing through the passion and rationality of Toegae (退溪, 心統性情論); etc. Scholarship is divided into two schools of thought. One school follows a theory in which the mind is just rationality (心則理說), the other asserts that the mind unifies passion and rationality (心合理氣說).³

Theory of Tai Chi (太極) and Yin Yang (陰陽)

In Chou I, the origin of the universe—and of all things—is Tai Chi

Figure 3-1
The Diagram of Eight Trigrams and Their Order of Fui
(伏羲八卦次序圖)

Chi Tzu Chuan said, "Chou I has Tai Chi (太極), Tai Chi creates Liang I (兩儀), Liang I create Ssu Hsiang (四象), Ssu Hsiang create Pa Kua (八卦)." Shao Tzu (邵子) said, "One divide into two, two divide into four, four divide into eight." Shuo Kuo Chauan (說卦傳) said, "Kan (乾) is 1, Tui (兌) is 2, Li (離) is 3, Chên (震) is 4, Hsün (巽) is 5, Kan (坎) is 6, Kên (艮) is 7, Kun (坤) is 8. From Kan to Kun ———."

Material: Kim, Hyuck Jae, 金赫濟, 上同, p.3.
         Kang, Chuen Bong, 退溪學報, 上同, 第四輯, p.108.

(太極). The creation function of Tai Chi is one of a continuous doubling. Two elements, Yin and Yang or Liang I (兩儀), arise from Tai Chi, four shapes, Ssu Hsiang (四象), arise from Liang I, and eight trigrams (八卦) arise from those four shapes. The theory of change is based on this creation.

Liang I (陰陽) stand against each other as strength and weakness; they push and pull each other, ultimately integrating with each other. Chi Tzu Chuan explains. "Tai Chi is in I Ching (易), Liang I originate from Tai Chi, SSU Hsiang originate from Liang I, Pa Kua (八卦) originate from SSu Hsiang."[4]

Fui Shih (伏羲氏) also showed the process of creation in the *Diagram of Eight Trigrams and Their Order* (伏羲八卦次序圖), and he wrote the explanation behind the diagram. There are two kinds of figures and explanations concerning Tai Chi. One is the Alternate Creation of Yin-Yang (陰陽生盛交替圖), which is known as ancient Tai Chi Tu (太極圖). The other is Ta Chi Tu, which connects the creation of Yin-Yang to the creation of all things. Ancient Tai Chi Tu was handed down through the doctrine school and it is known that Cho Jung Jeon transmitted this idea.[5] The direction and the position of pure Yin and pure Yang of ancient Tai Chi Tu coincides with the direction and the position of Fui Shih's *Direction Figure of Eight Trigrams* (伏羲八卦方位圖). Therefore, this theory seems to reflect the Tai Chi theory of Chou I.

Two types of ancient Tai Chi Tu were introduced. One was the Figure of the Alternate Creation of Yin-Yang, introduced in the book *Chi Meng Chuan I* (啟蒙傳疑). The other, called ancient Tai Chi Tu, was introduced by Han Dong Suek. According to the Figure of the Alternate Creation of Yin-Yang, two elements of strength (Yin and Yang) arose alternately in the middle position (Tai Chi) and expanded by pushing out the other elements of strength. When it became a period of pure Yin or pure Yang, they were pushed out by a newly-arising element of strength. Alternately, according to ancient Tai Chi Tu, two new elements of strength arose outside the other elements of strength and expanded by compressing those initial elements. When it became a period of pure Yin or pure Yang, they were shrunk by newly-arising and compressing elements of strength. These two ideas illustrate the same theory in the alternate creation of Yin-Yang, but with different directions and actions.

The meanings of the two ideas can be summarized. First, in the origin of universe, Tai Chi creates the Yin and the Yang alternately. Second, the relationship between Yin-Yang is a zero-sum relationship, so they check and balance each other. Third, the alternate creation of Yin-Yang is a continuous process of change, and is a circulating process. In other words, the period of pure Yin and pure Yang may not exist or it may be an extremely short period; they coexist in most times. Once Yang Chi (陽氣) expands and pushes out Yin Chi (陰氣), Yin Chi immediately begins to expand and pushes out Yang Chi. This is a function of Tai Chi that cannot be stopped or reversed. Two elements of strength, Yin Chi and Yang Chi, coexist and are interrelated. Even though the element looks like Yin Chi on the outside, Yang Chi overpowers Yin Chi on the inside or they confront tightly with each other.

Figure 3-2
The Alternate Creation Yin Yang (陰陽生盛交替圖)

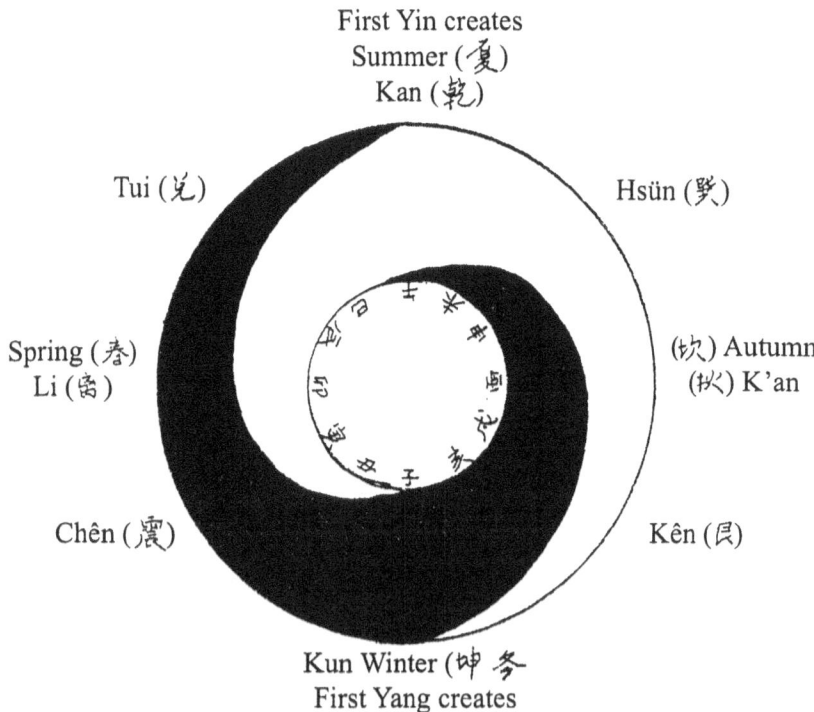

Material: Kang, Chuen Bong 姜天奉, "啓蒙傳疑研究", 退溪學報, 第七輯, 서울, 退溪學研究院, 1975, p.112.

Figure 3-3
Ancient Tai Chi Tu ((古) 太 極 圖)

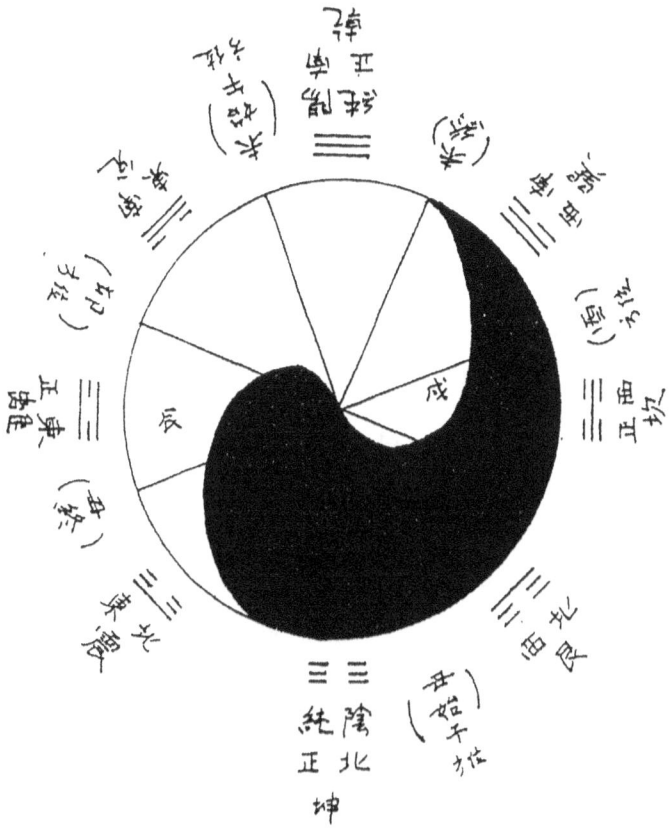

Material: Han, Dong Suek, ibid. p. 284

The period when Yang Chi starts to expand is expressed as thunder (震，雷，☳) and the period when Yang Chi pushes out Yin Chi—but when the strength of both elements are equivalent—is expressed as fire (離，火，☲). The period when Yang Chi overcomes Yin Chi is named pond (兌，澤，☱) and the period of pure Yang Chi is called heaven (乾，天，☰). The period when Yin Chi arises from inside and expands is expressed as wind (巽，風，☴) and the period when Yin Chi pushes out Yang Chi—but the strength of both elements are similar—is called water (坎，水，☵). The period when Yin Chi overcomes Yang Chi is called mountain (艮，山，☶) and the period of pure Yin Chi is called as earth (坤，地，☷).[6]

The theory of the alternate creation of Yin-Yang connects the creation of Yin-Yang with seasons and the ancient Tai Chi Tu connects the creation of Yin-Yang to direction. These two ideas of Tai Chi describe the relationship of Tai Chi and Yin-Yang very well, as was explained in *Chou I*. In the first chapter of *Upper Chi* Tzu Chuan said, "Heaven is high, earth is low, so it determines the Kan (乾) and Kun (坤), high and low determines the noble and ignoble, and the movement and stillness differentiate the sturdiness and weakness. The same kind of persons gather together according to their direction and divide into groups, good or bad is defined. Heaven creates the image and earth creates the shape, so it starts to change. Therefore the sturdiness conflicts with weakness, and eight trigrams create the lightening and thunder, and create the rain and wind, and movement of sun and moon alternate the coldness and hotness. The Kan way creates the male sex and the Kun way creates the female sex. The Kan perceives the truth and starts to create, and the Kun finishes the creation of all things."

In chapter 2 of *Upper Chi* Tzu Chuan expressed, "The sturdiness and the weakness pull each other and cause the change." All of these explanations analyzed the function of Yin-Yang. So Chou I explains all the changes through the Yin-Yang relationship.[7] From the movement of a celestial sphere to the creation of all things, it explains all changes of nature through the Yin-Yang relationship and the good or ill luck of human affairs. Nobleness—or the lack thereof—are also analyzed by the Yin-Yang relationship.

Tai Chi Tu, by Chou Lien Hsi (周濂溪，太極圖), reinforces the weakness of the ancient Tai Chi Tu and illustrates the creation of the five elements of strength and their functions. In the text of the Tae Chi Tu theory, Chou Lien Hsi described: "Wu Chi (無極) is Tai Chi (太極) (or Tai Chi come out from Wu Chi). Tai Chi moves and creates the Yang. When it moves extremely it becomes static and the static Tai Chi creates the Yin. When it becomes static extremely, it starts to move again. The alternation of one movement and one static divide the Yin and Yang, and they oppose and confront each other. Yang's variation and Yin's combination create the five elements (五氣)—the water (水), the fire (火), the wood (木), the metal (金), and the soil (土). The five elements (五氣，五行) cycle in regular order, so four seasons cycle too. The five elements are one of Yin-Yang, Yin-Yang is a Tai Chi, and Tai Chi is Wu Chi primarily. (The origin of Tai Chi is Wu Chi.)"[8]

In the explanation of the Tai Chi Tu, Chou Lien Hsi explained the Wu Chi theory (無極論). He showed the confrontation of the two elements and the creation of the five elements by the combination of two elements. In the explanation of the paragraph he states, "Wu Chi is Tai Chi (無極而太極)." Lu Hsiang Shan (陸象山) insisted that Tai Chi originated from the Wu Chi, but Chou Hsi (朱熹) explained that Wu Chi is Tai Chi, so Wu Chi and Tai Chi are the same being. Therefore, Tai Chi is not nothing but something.[9]

The question about which theory is right or wrong is not at the core of this analysis, so this question is postponed for future study. But both theories reached the same conclusion that Tai Chi is the origin of Yin-Yang and all things and that five elements are created by the relationship of Yin-Yang. The text of *Ta Chi Tu* continues: "Each part of Wu Hang (五行) has a particular characteristic. The sincerity of Wu Chi (無極的真) and the spirits of the two elements and the five elements (陰陽，水火木金土) coagulate in a peculiar way. A lump of the Kan element becomes male and a lump of the Kun element become female; two lumps of spirits respond to each other and create all things. This continuous creation causes the continuous change."[10]

The core of this description is that the spirit of Yin-Yang and Wu Hang join in a certain way and create the male and female who then interact with each other and create all things, but it does not describe the exact joining and sincerity of Yin-Yang and Wu Hang. However, the representation of sex means an appearance of a living organism; namely, that the actions of Wu Hang create the movements of the celestial sphere and the spirit of the two and five elements of strength create the living things. There are no understandable explanations about the sincerity of Wu Chi and the peculiar coagulation of the spirits of the two and five. Only Kim Il Bu (金一夫), who follows the theory of Lu Hsiang Shan that Tai Chi came out of Wu Chi, defined the relationship between Tai Chi and Wu Chi as a relationship of dissolution and unification. According to him, a situation of maximum dissolution (dispersion) to condition ten is a Wu Chi condition and a situation of maximum unification to condition one is a Tai Chi condition, so the relationship between Tai Chi and Wu Chi is a relationship between unification and dissolution. In the process of the creation of all things, the intermediation of the soil elements of strength is an essential factor. So he calls the position of the soil element Huang Chi (皇極), and thus connects the Tai Chi to the Wu Chi. But his theory is impossible to verify.[11]

Figure 3-4
Tai Chi Tu of Chou Lien Hsi (周濂溪의 太極圖)

The Wu Chi is the Tai Chi. (The Tai Chi comes out of the Wu Chi)
Tai Chi moves and creates the Yang. When it moves extremely it becomes static—the static Tai Chi creates the Yin. When it becomes static extremely it starts to move again. The alternation of movement and static divides the Yin and Yang, and they oppose and confront each other. Yang's variation and Yin's combination create the five elements— the water, the fire, the wood, the metal, the soil. These five elements circulate in regular order, so the four seasons rotate. The five elements are part of Yin-Yang, Yin-Yang are Tai Chi, and Tai Chi is primarily Wu Chi. Each of the five elements has a particular characteristic. The sincerity of Wu Chi and the spirit of the two and the five elements coagulate in a peculiar way, creating the lumps of elements. A lump of the Kan element becomes male and a lump of the Kun element becomes female—two lumps of spirit respond to each other and create all things. The continuous creation causes continuous change.

Material: Lee, Sang Eun, 李相殷 聖學十圖譯解, 서울, 退溪學研究院, 1982, p.14.

In any event, the Tai Chi Tu and its explanation can be summarized as follows: Tai Chi creates Yin-Yang and Yin-Yang creates Wu Hang (五行)—the water, the fire, the wood, the metal, and the soil. Wu Hang coagulated as a male lump of elements (Yang) and a female lump of elements of strength (Yin); these two lumps of elements of strength react with each other and create all things.

In other words, Tai Chi dissolves to Yin-Yang and Yin-Yang dissolves to Wu Hang. Wu Hang unites with Yin-Yang and Yin-Yang unites with Tai Chi. This continuous cycling of dissolution and unification is the creational function. They—Yang Chi (陽氣) and the Yin Chi (陰氣)—cannot create anything by themselves, but when they react with each other they can create something. The two elements of strength (兩氣) have opposite natures. Yang Chi is sturdy, active, and manly, so it marches forward. On the other hand, Yin Chi is docile, passive, and feminine, so it retreats always.

When Yang Chi marches forward and begins the creation process, Yin Chi reacts to Yang Chi and rides on (follow) Yang Chi. So Yang Chi starts creation and Yin Chi completes it. Numerically, Yang is an odd number and Yin is an even number. Yang means heaven and the way of the king, while Yin means earth and the way of the civilian.[12]

Tuan Tzu (彖辭), in the Kan and Kun hexagrams, described the nature of Yin and Yang. "Great! Kan Yuan (乾元)! All things originate from it. It goes with heaven. The cloud rises and the rain drops, so all things attain their shapes. When the beginning and the end are decided in time, and stroll about the heaven riding six dragons. Kan Tao (乾道) changes and straightens nature, preserves the great harmony. A saint controls all things so all the countries become peaceful." Tuan Tzu explained the Kan Tao and praised the great creative power of Yang I (陽儀).

Tuan Tzu in the Kun hexagram explained the nature of Yin I (陰儀). "Great! Kun Yuan (坤元)! All the things are originated from this. It obeys Yang's will docilely, it is thick enough to lead all things, and the infinite virtue is brightened widely and all things go well. A mare is a kind of earth so walk around the earth infinitely. The gentleness and rightness follow the king's virtue. If it leads the way it may lose the direction, but if it follows the Kan Tao it secures justice. Gaining friends in a southwestern direction means going with colleague."

"Though it loses friends in a northeastern direction, if it does the right thing, it will be good and peaceful. This means accommodating itself to the virtue of the earth."[13]

As shown in the previous description of Liang I, Yin and Yang have a conflicting relationship with each other. They push and pull each other, they oppose and combine with each other. But the conflict and opposition is not a negating relationship, but is a checking and constraining relationship for future unification. When Yin and Yang were created and grew, the constraining relationship prevented the overgrowth of Yin-Yang and maintained the balanced opposition for future unification. In other words, even though Yin and Yang push and pull each other, they do not negate but recognize each other.

According to Chi Tzu Chuan, "Kan Kun (乾坤) are main factors of change, so when Kan Kun are formed the change is completed. When Kan Kun collapse the change disappears; when there is no change, Kan Kun comes to an end."[14] This paragraph expresses the importance of Yin-Yang and their harmony.

Yin-Yang is heterogeneous and confront each other but they are not separate—they exist together. As the figure of the alternate creation of Yin-Yang shows, although Yin Chi is shown in outside seeing Yang Chi is growing in inside, and although Yang Chi is shown in outside seeing Yin Chi could overpower Yang Chi in inside. Therefore, Yin contains Yang and Yang contains Yin. The nature of the things created from the Yin-Yang union can have Yin, Yang, or neutral characteristics. When these things disperse or unite and create new things, this new creation is also a combined product of Yin and Yang.

The explanation of Tai Chi Tu states, "Wu Hang is one of Yin-Yang, and Yin-Yang is one of Tai Chi." Even though Tai Chi is divided into Yin-Yang, it is one with Tai Chi. And even though the interaction of Yin and Yang creates Wu Hang, the fire and the wood have the nature of Yang, the water and the metal have the nature of Yin, and the soil is neutral. These things also are Tai Chi and a combined product of Yin-Yang.[15]

Fui Shih's diagram of the eight trigrams and their order (伏羲八卦次序圖) and King Wen's figure of the eight trigrams and their order (文王八卦次序圖) show that Yin lines and Yang lines construct the trigrams, and that the trigrams are one with Yin-Yang.[16]

In chapter 4 of the *Lower Chi* Tzu Chuan explains, "The Yang trigram has more Yin lines and the Yin trigram has more Yang lines—how did it happened? The Yang trigram is odd numbered and Yin trigram is even numbered—what kind of virtue does it mean? The Yang trigram has one king and two civilians, so it is a way of a king. The Yin trigram has two kings and one civilian, so it is a way of a civilian." This explanation also shows that Yin and Yang construct the trigrams.[17]

The two elements of strength (Yang Chi 陽氣 and Yin Chi 陰氣) have an interchangeable nature. When Yang becomes extreme it changes into Yin and when Yin becomes extreme it transforms into Yang. This continuous interchangeability is called the mysteriously interchangeable action of the Yin-Yang (陰陽交流妙行). This is very similar to the theory of the alternate creation of the Yin-Yang and will be analyzed in the chapter about the Yang Pien Yin Hua (陽變陰化).

In the process of the creation of the Yin-Yang, the element which originated at the Yin was completed at the Yang and the thing which originated at the Yang was completed at the Yin, so it is almost impossible to handle the Yang and the Yin separately.

The Yang moves forward and the Yin moves backward, as was expressed in the explanation of the Ho Tu. The Yang moves forward from number 7 (young Yang) to number 9 (old Yang), and the Yin moves backward from number 8 (young Yin) to number 6 (old Yin). This phenomenon is called the common pattern of the Yin-Yang movement, or a norm of the advance and the retreat.

Interrelation between Yin-Yang is a zero-sum relationship. If the Yin increases, the Yang decreases; if the Yang increases, the Yin decreases. If the Yin is long, the Yang is short, and vice-versa. This phenomenon is shown in the illustration of the alternate creation of the Yin-Yang and in the length of day and night. The relationship between old Yin-Yang and young Yin-Yang is also a conflicting relationship—if old Yang prospers, young Yin declines. This phenomenon is called the Tich Wei Hsiao Chang of 7, 8, 9, 6 (迭為消長). But the conflicting relationship of the Yin-Yang is different from a general dialectic relationship. In the relationship of the Yin-Yang of Chou I, they conflict on one side and connect on the other side; they penetrate each other and they depend on each other. The Yin-Yang can be comprehended as noble and humble but cannot be comprehended as good or bad, and their relationship is not one of extreme struggling. It does not mean infinite advance or infinite retreat, it is not a relationship of negation of each other—the Yin-Yang relation is an infinitely circulating relationship.[18]

Theory of Ho Tu (河圖), Lo Shu (洛書) and the Origination of Wu Hang (五行)

The analysis of Ho Tu and Lo Shu is essential in order to understand the changing theory of Chou I. In the eleventh chapter of *Upper Chi Tzu Chuan* described that heaven created the divine thing and saints interpreted and showed the existence of four shapes. Chapter 9 divided the numbers shown in Ho Tu and Lo Shu into heaven's numbers and earth's numbers and described fully the principle and the method of Hsi Fa (筮法), which is the way to pick out the Kuo (卦) and construct the trigrams.[19]

Ho Tu is a diagram which came out from the Yellow River and Lo Shu is a letter which came out from the Lo River. According to the *Great Book of Change* (易大傳), a diagram came out from Yellow River and a letter came out from Lo River. Kung An Kuo (孔安國) wrote: "When Fui Shih (伏羲氏) was a king, he followed the pattern of the back style of a dragonhorse which came out of the Yellow River and drew the eight trigrams. Hsia Yu Shih (夏禹氏) embanked the Lo river; he found the numbers on the back of the mysterious tortoise who came out of the river, and granted Chiu Chou (九疇)."[20]

Ho Tu explains the unification principle of Yin and Yang through the odd and even numbers, and also shows the principle of the creation of Wu Hang (五行，水火木金土). Toegae explained the position of the numbers of Ho Tu and their creation. "When heaven (Yang) creates the water element with number 1, earth (Yin) completes this creation with number 6; when earth creates the fire element with number 2, heaven completes this with number 7; when heaven creates the wood element with number 3, earth completes this with number 8; when earth creates the metal element with number 4, heaven completes this with number 9; and when heaven creates the soil element with number 5, earth completes this with number 10."[21]

Ho Tu showed the mysterious function of the co-creation of Wu Hang. It starts at heaven's creation of the water element and shows the order of co-creation. "Heaven create the water element—The water element creates the wood element—The wood element creates the fire element—The fire element creates the soil element—The soil element creates the metal element—The metal element creates the water element." This relationship is shown in the illustration of the co-creation of Ho Tu. This diagram demonstrates that when winter turns to spring, the element of water (which contains the numbers 1 and 6) creates the element of

Figure 3-5
Ho Tu (河 圖)

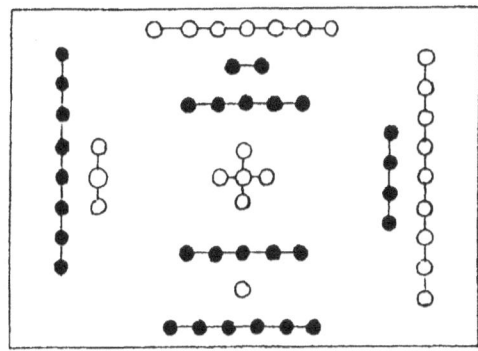

Figure 3-6
Lo Shu (洛 書)

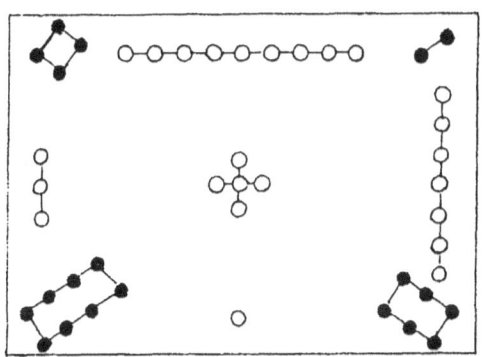

Material: Kim, Hyuck Jae, Chou I, ibid. p. 2

1, 2, 3, 4, and 5 are creation numbers and 6, 7, 8, 9, and 10 are completing numbers. Yang numbers are odd numbers and are expressed as a white circle, Yin numbers are even numbers and are expressed as a black circle. The Yin-Yang form of Ho Tu and Lo Shu is different depending upon their position, but the position of the soil is the same (in the middle).

wood (containing the numbers 3 and 8) and the element of wood creates the element of fire (numbers 2 and 7) in summer. The element of fire creates the element of soil (numbers 5 and 10) in mid-summer. The element of soil creates the element of metal (numbers 4 and 9) in autumn, and the metal element creates the element of water (numbers 1 and 6) in winter.

This diagram also shows the direction of Wu Hang.

Ho Tu shows the co-creation of the even numbers and odd numbers in the same place. On the other hand, Lu Shu shows the separation and the contradiction of Yin-Yang and Wu Hang. It starts at the bottom and shows the contradictory relationship of Yin-Yang and the reciprocal conquest of Wu Hang. "The water challenges the fire element, the fire element challenges the metal element, the metal element challenges the wood element, the wood element challenges the soil element, and the soil element challenges the water element." The challenge means the conflict or restraint. Han Dong Suek explained that this contradiction and restraint are essential conflicts for development and unification. He explained that all things are grown in the condition of contradiction and conflict and that conflict is essential for creation. For example: In order to maintain its shape and to create the element of fire, the element of wood should be challenged by the element of metal; in order to maintain its shape and to create the element of soil, the element of fire should be challenged by the element of water; in order to maintain its shape and to create the element of metal, the soil should be challenged by the element of wood; in order to maintain its shape and to create the element of water, the element of metal should be challenged by the element of fire; and in order to maintain its shape and to create the element of wood, the element water should be challenged by the soil element.

So there is no creation or growth of all things without conflict, and conflict and contradiction are essential for change.[22]

In the creation of Wu Hang there is not only the co-creation and the co-challenge, but also the co-insult and the co-rearing. If a challenger is not strong enough to win in a co-challenging situation, the challenger becomes insulted. Therefore, the co-insulting relationship effects the opposite direction of the co-challenge. In a co-creation condition, a new creature can grow with the nutrition of the old one, so the old one becomes weak. This kind of relationship is called a co-rearing relationship.

When all of these functions of creation are synthesized, we can generalize the function of Wu Hang. "The element of water creates the element of wood, but in the process of creation the water element is created by the metal element, is challenged from the soil element, is insulted by the fire element, and is reared by the wood element. Therefore, a creation accompanies the co-challenge, the co-insult, and the co-rearing.

Figure 3-7
The Co-Creation of Ho Tu (河圖相生圖 (順類))

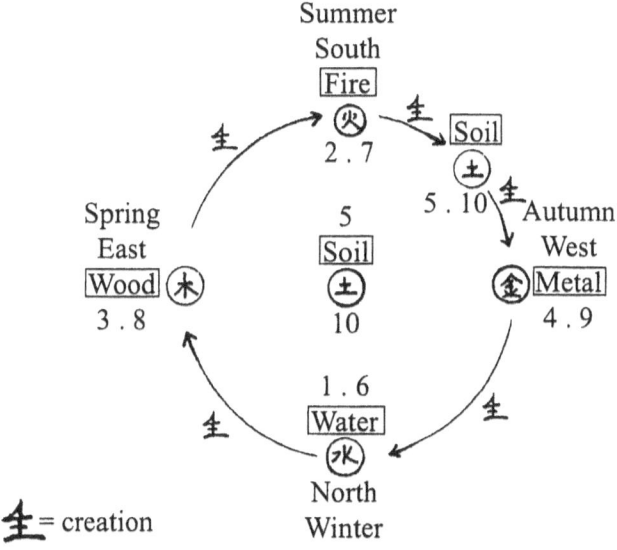

生 = creation

Material: Kang, Chuen Bong, 姜天奉, 退溪學報 第三輯, p.128. p.91.
Han, Dong Suek, 韓東錫, 宇宙變化의 原理. 上同.

Figure 3-8
The Co-Challenge of Lo Shu (洛書相克, 正陽圖)

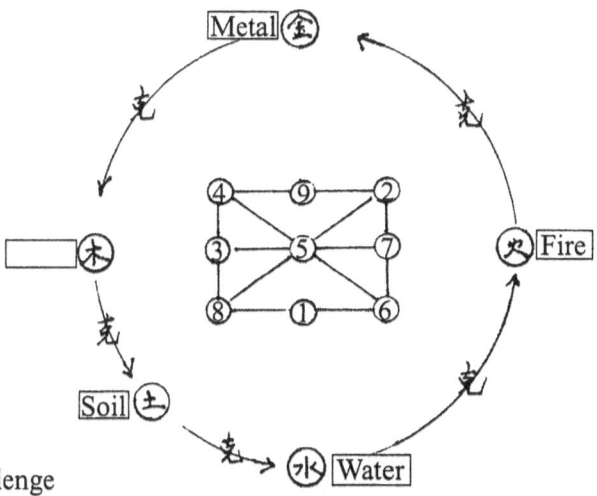

克 = challenge

Material: Kang, Chuen Bong, 姜天奉, 退溪學報 第三輯, pp.89.91.128.

"The five elements—the water (水), the fire (火), the wood (木), the metal (金), and the soil (土)—all have different characteristics.

According to Toegae, the wood element (木氣) belongs to benevolence (仁), its gender is young Yang (少陽), its nature is soft (柔軟). According to Han Dong Suek, the wood element means strong power in which an accumulated Yang element gushes out from inside. When it arises, it encounters the surrounded pressure. The stronger the surrounding pressure is, the stronger the gushing force is. So the wood element arises from the struggle between the pressure and the repulsion. In other words, the wood element is the Yang element that is escaping from the congealed water elements in spring time, so its age is young boyhood.[23]

According to Toegae, the fire element (火氣) belongs to courtesy (禮), its gender is great Yang (太陽), its body is dark, its nature is intense, and it comes out of the sun heat."[24] According to Han Dong Suek, the fire element receives strength from the wood element and disperses it, so the strength weakens. Its season is summer and its age is young (青年期).

According to Toegae, the metal element (金氣) belongs to righteousness (義), meaning achievement, and the metal element is created from the dry element. Its gender is young Yin (少陰), its body is bright, and its nature is strong.[25] According to Han Dong Suek, the metal element acts in the opposite direction of the wood element. It stops the wood element's variation to the fire element. It surrounds the Yang element and induces fruiting. Its season is autumn and its age is prime manhood.

According to Toegae, the water element (水氣) belongs to intelligence (智), it completes the congealment, and controls life or death. When the Yin element is extreme, the cold element arises and the water element is created from the chilliness. Its gender is great Yin (太陰), its body is light, and its nature is quiet.[26] According to Han Dong Suek, when the metal element stores the Yang element, the water element congeals this deeply; its season is winter and its age is old. The water element has the nature of coagulation, autonomy, and medium, so it is a basic element of creation and the complete congealment means the complete creation (fruit).

According to Toegae, the soil element (土氣) belongs to confidence (信)—the confidence comes from the sincerity, the sincerity should be straight. The soil element is in the middle position of the five elements and it manages the creation of the five elements. The Yin-Yang in the middle co-reacts with each other and creates the moistures, which in turn create the soil element. The soil element generally has no gender and enjoys the co-remedy depending on the season change. The body of the soil element contains four elements (水，火，木，金), and it contains truth and falsehood together. The water and the metal show the Yin nature and the wood and the fire show the Yang nature, but the soil shows the neutral nature.[27] According to Han Dong Suek, the soil element mediates the fire and metal elements. The growing nature of the fire element and the containing nature of the metal element conflict with each other, so the metal element cannot contain the fire element without the mediation of the soil element. Therefore, the mediation of the co-struggle between the fire element and the metal element (金火相爭) is the nature of the soil element.

Han Dong Suek introduced the particular system of logics about the creation of the five elements. He defined the reason for the five elements as a dispersion and unification movement of Tai Chi. The concentrated Yang element starts to disperse in spring and creates the wood element, but it should be powerful enough to break through the surrounding pressure. When the pressure increases on the wood element, it displays its strength, gushing out power and breaking through the resistance, thus creating the fire element. The fire element succeeds the wood element and leads the growth. In summer, the fire element succeeds the wood element and leads the growth. In summer, the fire element accomplishes the maximum dispersion.

The wood element and the fire element break out of the concentrated Yang element from inside. In this process the aid and restraint of the soil element is an essential factor. This function is called the Wood-Fire-Soil Action (木火土作用). At the summer solstice, the hottest time of summer, the fire element creates the soil element and the soil element creates the metal element. The metal element has a Yin nature, which suppresses the growth and unifies the elements. Because of this nature, the metal element intensely conflicts with the fire element. This phenomenon is called the co-struggle of the metal element and the fire element (金火相爭). In general, the metal element contains the fire element. This containment is impossible without the mediation of the soil element. It is in autumn during which all things stop growing and begin to fruit.

After the containment, the metal element creates the water element. In this containment and unification of the metal element and water element, the help of the soil element is an essential factor. The season of this action is winter.

The reason why the Yin element unifies with the Yang element is for the completion of creation. He defined this entire process as a repeating and circulating process and as a principle of change of the universe. In other words, the principle of the change of all things and the universe is a continuous circulation and alternation of the Wood-Fire-Soil Movement (木火土作用) and the Metal-Water-Soil movement (金水土作用). The wood and the fire are Yang in nature and the metal and the water are Yin in nature. So this process is a repeating or circulation of the Yin-Yang. In this process there are co-creation, co-struggle, co-insulting, and co-rearing phenomena, and the absolutely neutral element (soil) aids and protects the creation process. So Kim Il Bu gives the name "Emperor pole (皇極)" to the soil element.[28]

He also asserted the abnormal movement of the five elements of strength in the earth. The dispersion of Tai Chi and the unification of the five elements of strength are normal motions of the five forces of strength. But the creation of all things and the change of the earth is an abnormal movement which favors the Yang element more than the Yin element—in a 3:2 ratio— because the axis of the earth leans about 23.7 degrees. Over-allocation of the Yang element creates one more fire element, called Co-fire (甲寅相火), so the five elements become six elements.[29]

Because the movements of the five elements of strength and the movements of the six elements of strength mismatch, there are endless changes in the earth. Furthermore, the declination of the axis of the earth appears in the over-Yang phenomenon. It makes the unification function of Yin difficult; the exchange of the metal element into the fire element (金火交易) creates all the vices on the earth. Fortunately, according to him, the soil element in the middle—the Emperor Pole—mediates the conflicts and struggles and helps the unification process. Therefore, he concluded that the movement of the universe is a movement in which the soil element of strength passes through the co-fire phenomenon (相火現象) and completes the exchange of the metal element into the fire element.

The validity of the theory of Han Dong Suek cannot be verified, but his theory is the only one which this writer can find which explains "the sincerity of Wu Chi" in the explanation of Tai Chi Tu. (Each of Wu Hang has one particular characteristic. The sincerity of Wu Chi and the spirits of two elements and five elements coagulate in a peculiar way.) Han

The Theory of Change 51

Dong Suek's theory coincides with the figure of the direction of the eight trigrams of King Wen and with the Shuo Kua Chuan (說卦傳). The position and the order of the wood, the fire, the metal, and the water in Han Dong Suek's theory coincides with the figure of the direction of the eight trigrams of King Wen.

Figure 3-9
The Direction of Eight Trigrams of King Wen (文王八卦 方位圖)

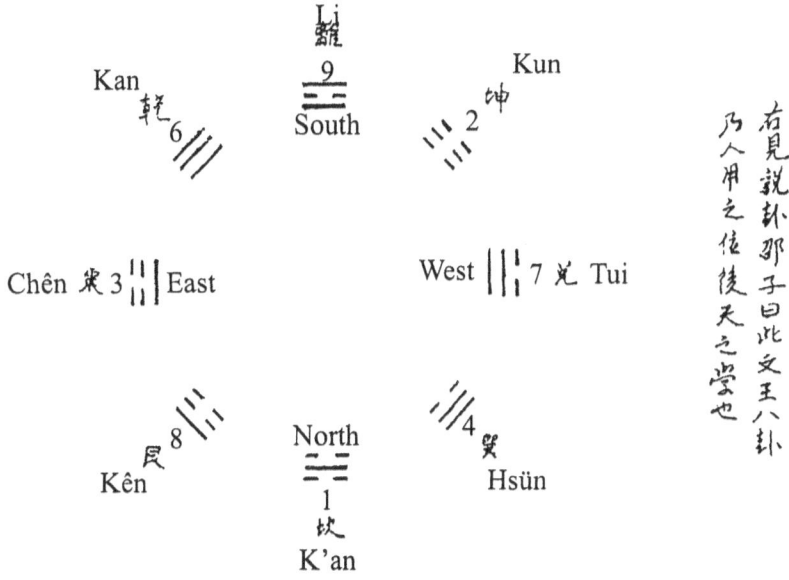

Material: Kim Hyuck Jae,
Sim, Jong Chuel, 金赫濟, 周易, 本義圖説 p.6., 沈鍾哲, 上同, p.10.

Chapter 5 of *Shuo Kua Chuan* of Chou I explained the direction and the functions of the five elements. "The strong element, Yang Chi (陽氣), is divined as the emperor. The emperor comes out from the east (震) during spring, when all things start to grow, symmetrizes all the created things on the wind's direction (巽方, southeast) during the mild season between spring and summer, watches the shape of all the created things in the south (離方) during the hot, growing summer season, and labors to cultivate all things in the southwest (坤方) between summer and autumn. It enjoys the harvest in the west (兌方) during cool autumn, when all things ripen, harmonizes the co-struggle of the two elements of Yin-Yang in the northwest (乾方) between autumn and winter, stands the toil of the coldness in the north during winter when all the things rest and store, and sprouts all the dead things in the northeast (艮方) between winter and spring.

"All the things originate from the thunder (震), so the thunder belongs to spring and it means the east direction. 'Making evenly at the wind (巽)' means that the wind symmetrizes all things in a south- eastern direction, so 'making evenly' means a symmetrical arrangement. The fire element (離) is so vigorous in the southern direction that all things brighten. A saint sits toward the south, listens to all the political happenings, and leads the people toward the right direction—all these actions are in imitation of the image of trigram. The earth (坤) means 'ground,' so grows all things in a southeastern direction and labors on the earth's direction. The delight of the pond direction (兌方) means enjoyment of the maturity of all things in autumn; the fighting at the heaven direction (乾方) means that the heaven is a northwestern trigram, so two elements (Yin-Yang) are fighting when autumn turns to winter. The water (坎) is a painful trigram that contains all of the water element in the northern direction. Because all things are stored and the emperor withstands the chilly difficulties, it works hard at the water trigram.

"The mountain (艮) is a concluding trigram in the northeast direction. Therefore, it concludes in the mountain's direction and starts a new circulation. This is the theory of the action of the post-heaven trigram (後天八卦) which was described in the chapter of *Shuo Kua Chuan*."[30]

The above explanation in *Shuo Kua Chuan* is that the five elements (the wood, the fire, the water, the metal, the soil) act upon the changes of the four seasons. Therefore, the theory of the five elements of Han Dong Suek seems to follow the theory in *Shuo Kua Chuan*. But in the direction and order of *Shuo Kua Chuan*, the theory is not fitted to a real situation, so there are many subjects left for future study.

There are many plants which germinate in spring and fruit in summer in which the Yang element is highest, and there are many plants which germinate in autumn and fruit in spring. There are many cycles of the dispersion and the unification in animal life—one-, three-, and six-month cycles, plus other cycles which can last many decades—so these cycles are not coincident with the four seasons. Furthermore, many perennial plants repeat the growth and standstill for many years and fruiting does not coincide with seasons. Tropical plants repeat the dispersion and the unification continuously. So these kinds of variations cannot be analyzed by the traditional Yin-Yang relationship.

The axis theory of Han Dong Suek is a very questionable theory. The theory in which the axis of the earth transfers according to a cycle cannot be validated until the axis of the earth transfers in reality. Even if the axis of the earth does transfer, it does not seem to cause the over-Yang phenomenon on the surface of the earth. The co-effect of the magnetic action of the earth and sunlight may create certain circumstances. This is a good subject of study, but it seems to be difficult to relate the declination of the axis of the earth to over-Yang phenomenon. Therefore, the theory of the five elements' movement (五運運動理論) cannot be generalized through the seasonal or directional changes.

Change Theory of Chou I (周易)

The basic principle of the change theory of Chou I is the alternate creation of Yin-Yang from the Tai Chi and the creation of all things through the unification of the Yin and Yang. But depending upon the method of analysis, it can be differentiated into six concepts—the creation, the Yang Pien Yin Hua, the cycling order, the harmonious unification, the balance, and the stability.

The creation means that creation is a change by itself; the Yang Pien Yin Hua refers to the co-exchange that when Yang becomes extreme it turns to Yin and when Yin becomes extreme it turns to Yang. The cycling order is a repeating change upon the cycle, just like the movement of a celestial sphere and harmonious unification means the harmonious unification of the Yin-Yang. Balance means a balanced structure of the Yin-Yang and stability means maintenance of the system.

Creation

According to chapter 5 of the *Upper Chi Tzu Chuan* (繫辭上傳), creation is a change by itself and chapter 1 of the *Lower Chi Tzu Chuan* (繫辭下傳) said, "The great virtue of the heaven and earth is creation."
[31] It means that the virtue of nature is a creation and the goal of the celestial movement of Tai Chi is creation. Creation is a kind of change by itself and the creation is a cause of a change.

Creation is possible when Yin and Yang are harmonized. Two elements of strength, Yin and Yang, can oppose each other and conflict with each other, but when they unify creation is complete. As described in chapter 1, creation starts from the movement of Tai Chi.

In the explanation of Tai Chi Tu, the alternation of the movement and rest of Tai Chi creates two elements of strength, Yin and Yang (陰陽), and Yin-Yang creates five elements of strength (五氣，水火木金土) through the Yang Pien Yin Ho process (陽變陰合). The two elements, the five elements, and the sincerity of Wu Chi (無極的真) create the male and female bundles of elements. The reaction of these two masses of elements creates all things and the continuous process of this reaction is called the continuous creation. The creation and the disappearance of things cause change, and the increase and the decrease of things are changes by themselves.[32]

Han Dong Suek, who followed the theory of Kim Il Bu, analyzed this process as a dispersion and unification. The process of dispersion is that Tai Chi becomes Yin-Yang and Yin-Yang becomes Wu Hang; the process of unification is that Wu Hang becomes Yin-Yang and Yin-Yang becomes Tai Chi. In other words, Tai Chi disperses to Wu Hang and they restore to Tai Chi.[33]

The next fact is that each Wu Hang has its own particular nature but also appear with a Yin-Yang nature and show the nature of Tai Chi. The movement of Tai Chi creates Yin-Yang but Yin-Yang is not a completely separated something, as Yin-Yang are themselves another form of Tai Chi and the five elements create a thing by peculiar combination—this thing is also a Tai Chi. On the other hand, Kim Il Bu defined the Tai Chi as a condition of maximum unification and Wu Chi as a condition of maximum dispersion. So Kim's theory is different from Chou Lien Hsi's theory (周濂溪的太極論). One basic question arises at this point: Is the goal of nature a continuous growth or a circulation which repeats the dispersion and unification?

The conflict between Yin-Yang and the unification of Yin-Yang were mentioned in several places. In the explanation about the creation of the eight trigrams, Toegae explained, "The creation is accomplished after Yin and Yang co-react and combine with each other. Old Yang reacts to old Yin and young Yang reacts to young Yin. Therefore, as the father and mother face each other, the son and daughter-in-law also face each other."
[34] So the original goal of the Yin-Yang relationship is a creation and this goal can be accomplished by the unification of Yin and Yang.

Chi Tzu Chuan also explains the theory of the Yin-Yang union. Chapter 4 of the *Upper Chi Tzu Chuan* introduced the letter, "Knowing the death and life through the observation of the origin and the end (原始反終故知死生之說)." Sim Jong Chuel explained it as: "When Yin and Yang combine, life starts; when Yin and Yang separate, life ends. So one can find the question of the life and death." He also introduced the theory of Wang Fu Fa (清的王夫之): "Death does not mean nothing-ness. Life means an accomplishment of Yin-Yang change and death means turning back to the original condition. So death does not mean extinction."[35] Therefore, it is clear that the Yin-Yang union means life.

Furthermore, chapter 5 of the *Lower Chi Tzu Chuan* said, "By the entanglement of the heaven and the earth all the things are transformed, and by the reaction of male and female all things are created. The I (易) said, 'If three persons go together they will lose one, and if one goes he will get one friend.'"[36] This means that the unification of Yin and Yang create all things.

Tuan Tzu of the Hsien hexagram (咸卦) described, "By the reaction of the heaven and the earth, all the things are generated."[37] This means that all things can be generated by the reaction of the Yin and Yang. The Tuan Tzu of the Kwei Mei hexagram (歸妹卦) explained, "Kwei Mei is the great meaning of the heaven and the earth—if heaven and earth do not unite all things will not prosper, so Kwei Mei is a beginning of human beings and a final end."[38] Kwei Mei means a marriage in which Yin and Yang unify. This marriage is a law of nature—if heaven and earth do not unify, all things will not be created; if male and female do not react and combine, there will be no descendants. Therefore, the harmonious unification of Yin and Yang is important.

This is of great importance. So called, the life has its life by the combination of Yin and Yang, and if Yin-Yang is dispersed it loses the life and dies. This principle can be applied not only to a living body but also to the spirit.[39] The unification of Yin and Yang is a generation; therefore, the unification of Yin and Yang has great meaning and it is a great virtue of nature.

The theory of the creation of the eight trigrams also shows the principle of the Yin-Yang union. Fui Shih's diagram and King Wen's diagram of the creation of the eight trigrams are different. In Fui Shih's diagram of the creation of the Yin-Yang, the lines of the Yin-Yang pile up from 2 to 4, and from 4 to 8; in King Wen's diagram, the creation of first daughter, middle daughter, and young daughter, and the creation of first son, middle son, and young son from their parents is shown. This expresses that the heaven (Yang) and the earth (Yin) operate as major factors in the creation of nature and that the male and the female operate as major factors in the generation of a human being.

Figure 3-10
The Direction of the Creation of Eight Trigrams of Fui Shih
伏羲八卦生成方位圖

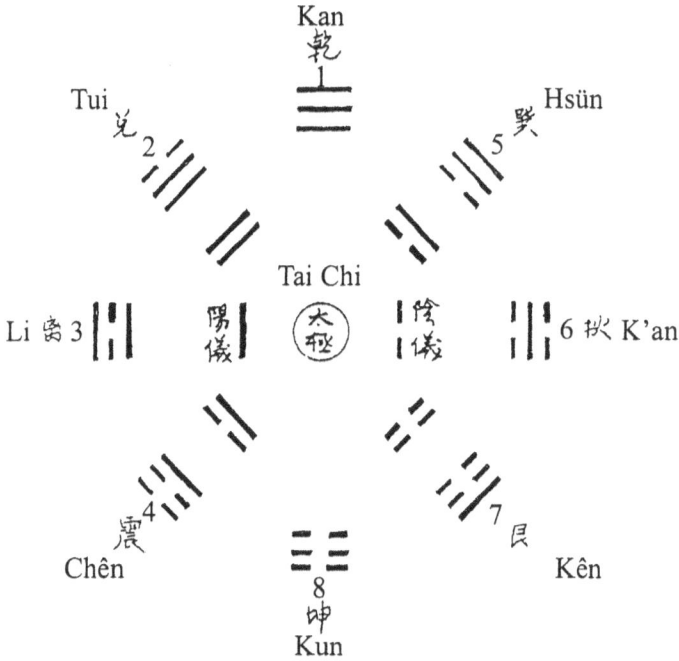

Material: Kang, Chuen Bong, 姜天奉, 退溪學報 第五・六輯, p.180

Chu Tzu's (朱子) theory and Tung Shih's (董氏) theory differ in the creation of the eight trigrams. According to Toegae, "The harmonious reaction of Yin-Yang can be completed after they unite with each other and finish the creation. The old Yang intercourses with the old Yin and the young Yang intercourses with young Yin. In other words, just as the father faces the mother, the son faces the daughter-in-law according to the same moral principle."

The Theory of Change 57

Depending on the subjectivity of the Yin-Yang relationship, the gender of the created thing varies. According to Chu Tzu, Yin intercourses with Yang and creates Yin, and Yang intercourses with Yin and creates Yang. Thus Chu Tzu's emphasis on the subject of intercourse. On the other hand, Tung Shih's emphasis is on the object of intercourse. According to Tung Shih, Yang intercourses with Yin and creates Yin and Yin intercourses with Yang and creates Yang. These theories also demonstrate that the intercourse between Yin and Yang and the unification of Yin-Yang are functions of creation.

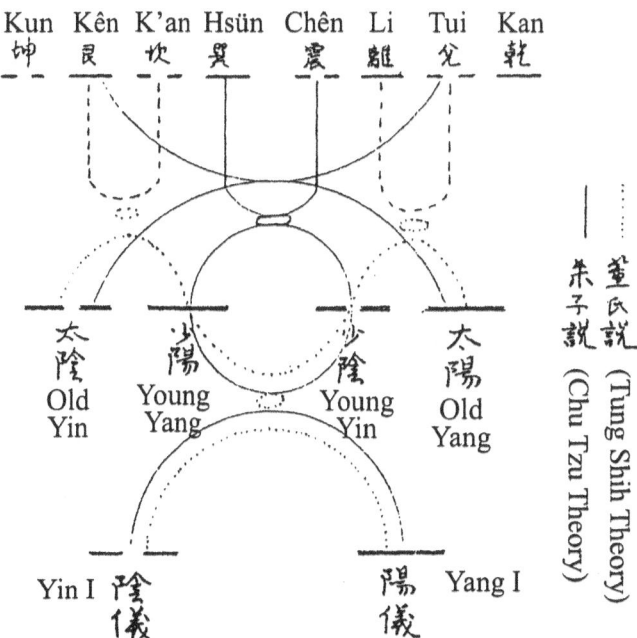

Figure 3-11
Chu Tzu's Theory and Tung Shih's Theory
朱子說圖와 董氏說圖

Material: Kang Chuen Bong, 姜天奉, 退溪學報 第五・六輯, p.182.184

In the theory of the creation of the five elements (五行), Toegae used the same principle of the Yin-Yang relationship. In the explanation of Ho Tu (河圖), Toegae explained the Yin-Yang unification in two separate processes of creation. "The odd numbers 1, 3, 5, 7, and 9, which have the nature of the Yang, intercourse with the even numbers 2, 4, 6, 8, and 10, which have the nature of the Yin. When heaven creates the water element with number 1, the earth completes this with number 6; when the earth creates the fire element with number 2, heaven completes this with number 7; when heaven creates the wood element with number 3, the earth completes this with number 8; when the earth creates the metal element with number 4, heaven completes this with number 9; when heaven creates the soil element with number 5, the earth completes this with number 10." These theories can be generalized as: "The origin of the creation and change is Tai Chi. The Yin-Yang comes out of Tai Chi and Wu Hang comes out of Yin-Yang, and all things come out of Wu Hang. But the things can be created by the unification of Yin-Yang. Life comes from the unification of Yin-Yang and death comes from the dispersion of Yin-Yang. Therefore, creation is a great virtue of nature and creation is good in value claim."

Even though the creation and unification of Yin-Yang is an important function for creation, the nature of Yin-Yang is different and there are some conflicts between Yin and Yang in the process of creation. This conflicting relationship cannot be treated as a bad phenomenon; it is a necessary vice for creation. Kim Il Bu defined the Yin-Yang relationship as a contradictory and conflicting one and treated it as a required condition for development. Han Dong Suek, who followed the theory of Kim Il Bu, regarded the conflict and struggle of Yin-Yang as a phenomenon of advance and retreat (advance for retreat or retreat for advance). According to him, "The goal of heaven's movement is creation. In order to accomplish this a Yin shape (陰形), which protects the Yang pole (陽極), is required. Even though the Yin shape carries out this important aim, it has an enemy-like relationship with the Yang element. The Yin and Yang have a conflicting relationship (相克關係) and this conflict is necessary and an essential vice of nature."[40]

Chou I did not use the word "struggle," but expressed the co-reaction, or transition (推移), in the explanation of the conflicting relationship. Chapter 1 of the *Upper Chi Tzu Chuan* expressed the conflicting relation of Yin-Yang like this: "The heaven is high and the earth is low, so Yin Yang is defined. When high and low are defined, the nobleness and the humbleness are decided; when the movement and rest occur normally, the sturdiness and mildness are decided; when same kinds gather together by direction and the groups are differentiated, the good or ill luck is defined; when heaven makes an image and earth makes a shape, the change follows them; when sturdiness and mildness rub each other, eight trigrams start to act."[41] So *Chi Tzu Chuan* expressed contrary concepts such as heaven and earth, high and low, noble and humble, movement and rest.

Chapter 2 of *Upper Chi Tzu Chuan* and chapter 1 of *Lower Chi Tzu Chuan* described that the sturdiness and the mildness push each other and bring about change. Chapter 5 of the *Lower Chi Tzu Chuan* explained the conflicting relationship of Yin-Yang. "When the sun is down, the moon is up, and when the moon is down, the sun is up, so the sun and moon create the light by pushing each other. The chillness goes, the hotness comes, and when the hotness goes the chillness comes, and the chillness and hotness fill up a year by pushing each other, a bending means going and a straightening is coming, so a bending and a straightening create the benefit by reacting with each other." So *Chi Tzu Chuan* explains that the conflicting relationship of Yin-Yang is natural, and the relationship of the pusher and the pushed is essential for creation.[42]

There are many assertions that the conflicting relationship is a necessary phenomenon in the *Chou I*. According to Chapter 5 of the *Lower Chi Tzu Chuan*, "There are many ways to go in the world, but the final goal is the same one; there are hundreds of thoughts, but the final accomplishment is the same. Why worry? The reason a looper bends is for stretching."[43] This means that the Yin and the Yang are divided and conflicted, but that all these happenings are for creation—a goal of Tai Chi. Kang, Chuen Bong expressed this phenomenon. "Yin and Yang harmonize as each other on one side, but substitute as opposition on the other side."[44]

The Shih Ho (噬嗑) hexagram and the Kuei (睽) hexagram also expressed creation through conflict and friction. Tuan Tzu of the Shih Ho hexagram (噬嗑卦的彖辭) says, "Something in the mouth means chewing together, go well by chewing together. The sturdiness and mildness divides and lightens by moving, and lightening are united and splendid."[45] By this, Tuan Tzu means that friction is essential for creation. Tuan Tzu of Kuei (睽卦的彖辭) says, "The fire moves upward, the pond moves downward. Two daughters live together but their minds are not accord. Enjoys and depends on the clarity, progresses gently and goes upward, attains the middle and responds to the sturdiness. Therefore, it brings good luck in only small matters. The heaven and earth mismatch on the road but their goals are same. Man and woman are opposites but their spirit communicates with each other. All beings of the world stand in opposition to one another but their final aim is accord, so the time and the usage of Kuei is great!" This paragraph explains that even though antagonism and opposition are not good nor lucky, there is a common end of Tai Chi inside them.[46]

The change is described as a positive, essential one in *Chou I*. Chapter 2 of the *Lower Chi Tzu Chuan* lectures, "After Shen Nung Shih (神農氏) died, emperor Yao (堯) and Shun (舜) came out and made things work by using change, encouraged people to not be idle, and inspired the people to do right things. So when change is needed it will change—when it changes, it does so thoroughly, and lasts for a long time."[47]

The phrases, "when change is needed, it will change," and, "teach the people through the change," express that change is an essential fact in nature. The last chapter of the *Lower Chi Tzu Chuan* describes, "The change is a beneficial thing; the good and ill luck means a transference of passion. Therefore, the conflict between affection and enmity creates good and ill luck, the interreaction of truth and false creates gain and loss. In general, the passion is very near; if not felt together, it brings ill luck and loss, so feel remorseful and feel shameful."[48] According to *Chi Tzu Chuan*, the conflicts between love and hatred, between remoteness and closeness, and between truth and false, create good or ill luck; remorse and resentment, gain and loss, and change are essential and beneficial things.

Not only *Chi Tzu Chuan*, but also the Kun hexagram (坤卦), the Chi Chi hexagram (既濟卦), and the Ku hexagram (蠱卦) insist upon the necessity of change. The Kun hexagram explains change. "When heaven and earth change, all the plants and trees flourish. But when heaven and earth close, wise men hide. Therefore, when heaven and earth close, the thoughts of kings and servants do not come to a mutual understanding." In the explanation of the Chi Chi hexagram, Sim Jone Chuel said, "All the lines of the Chi Chi hexagram respond at the right position, so it seems to be the ideal hexagram. But the excellence of the Yin-Yang relationship comes out of irregularity. So I (易) means continuous change and continuous development."[49] In the explanation of the Ku hexagram, Sim Jong Chuel also insisted, "If peace continues, corruption and disorder arise from inside and correction of the disorder is a dangerous thing. But once society is out of order it should begin recovery—it is a law of nature."[50] He insists on the necessity of change again.

The theories of the creation of the Chou I have been analyzed and summarized; many theories connected to Chou I have been analyzed to this point. Some questionable points needing more study will be generalized in the next chapter. All the other theories about origination can be summarized as follows.

First, the origin of all things in the universe is Tai Chi. Tai Chi creates the Yin-Yang, the Yin-Yang creates the Wu Hang, and the Wu Hang creates all things. Second, the creating function means the appearance of the Yin-Yang from Tai Chi and their unification. The appearance of the Yin-Yang is a creation (生), and the unification of the Yin-Yang is a completion (成). Third, two elements of strength, the Yin element (陰氣) and the Yang element (陽氣), have different natures, so they confront each other and conflict with each other. But they do not negate each other. Instead, they communicate with and subsidize each other; they complete creation by uniting at a decisive time. Fourth, the movement and rest of Tai Chi and the creation of the Yin-Yang is a natural phenomenon which cannot be stopped artificially—it is a great virtue of nature and it is good. Fifth, the creating function is a change by itself and is a cause of change. Continuous creation causes continuous change. Therefore, change is inevitable and is good. Finally, the creating function of Tai Chi and Yin-Yang change not only nature, but also humans and human society. This phenomenon can be explained two ways but the basic principles are the same. One is that human beings repeat the life and death cycle as a part of nature. Another is that human beings repeat the creation and the dispersion of the human groups in human society. The continuous generation and death of human beings continuously change human beings and human society. All the changes that were described previously occur according to a uniform principle and this principle does not change.

Yang Pien Yin Hua (陽變陰化)

According to the theory of the alternate creation of the Yin-Yang, the Yin element and the Yang element are created alternately and the repetition of the alternate creation causes change. This kind of phenomenon is sometimes called the Yang Pien Yin Hua theory. It is a theory stating that when the Yang element is extreme it turns to the Yin element and when the Yin element is extreme it turns to the Yang element, and that the Yang element is inside the Yin element and the Yin element is inside the Yang element. Therefore, Yang Pien Yin Hua theory contains somewhat different meanings from the alternate creation theory of the Yin-Yang.

When we scrutinize the Figure of the Alternate Creation of the Yin-Yang, we find that at a particular time it looks like a Yin element on the outside with the Yang element growing inside; it looks like a Yang element from the outside looking in, but the Yin element is growing inside.

This finding has two important meanings. One is that the Yin element and the Yang element lie together at the same time in the same place. The other is that when the Yang element is extreme, the Yin element starts to grow, and when the Yin element is extreme, the Yang element start to grow. This phenomenon supports the theory that when the Yang element is extreme it turns into the Yin element and when the Yin element is extreme it turns into the Yang element.[51] But the writings in the book described this as if the materials of the Yang or Yin elements change into the materials of the Yin or Yang element. Also, the explanation of the changing action is different from that of the circulation or repetition of Yin-Yang or Wu Hang. Therefore, the Yang Pien Yin Hua theory is treated separately.

There are two theories of Yang Pien Yin Hua. One is the theory of the mysterious interchanging (交流妙行論) and the other is the theory of the flying and hiding mystery (飛伏神理論). The theory of the mysterious interchanging is in *Chi Tzu Chuan*. Chapter 9 of the *Upper Chi Tzu Chuan* describes: "Heaven's number is 1, earth's number is 2; heaven's number is 3, earth's number is 4; heaven's number is 5, earth's number is 6; heaven's number is 7, earth's number is 8; heaven's number is 9, earth's number is 10. Heaven has 5 numbers and earth has 5 numbers. The sum of the five heaven numbers is 25 and the sum of the five earth numbers is 30. The sum of both heaven's and earth's numbers is 55. These fifty-five numbers make the change and do the mysterious behaviors of Kuei Shen (鬼神)." Toegae explained this mystery of the numbers. "Number 1 changes into the water element, number 6 completes its transformation; number 2 transforms into the fire element, number 7 completes its change; number 3 changes into the wood, element number 8 completes its transformation; number 4 transforms into the metal element, number 9 completes its change; number 5 changes into the soil element, number 10 completes its transformation."[52]

This explanation insists that the harmonious unification of the odd—heaven's numbers 1, 3, 5, 7, and 9—and the even—earth's numbers 2, 4, 6, 8, and 10—accomplishes the mysterious creation of all beings, and explains that the numbers 1 and 6, 2 and 7, 3 and 8, 4 and 9, and 5 and 10 unify each other in a harmonious way. In this explanation, the changes of the heaven's numbers are expressed as Pien (變) and the transformation of the earth numbers are expressed as Hua (化). The change of the Yang numbers are expressed as Pien (變) and the change of the Yin numbers are expressed as Hua (化).

Kang Chuen Bong explained the mysterious interchange (交流妙行). "In general, Yin-Yang has a principle of change that acts reciprocally and shares the mutual relationship. When Yang is extreme it changes into Yin and when Yin is extreme it transforms to Yang. Yang contains Yin and Yin contains Yang. Things created at Yang complete their creation at Yin and things created at Yin complete their creation at Yang. This reciprocal action is an endless alternation called the mysterious interchanging of Yin-Yang."[53]

The theory of the alternate creation of Yin-Yang and the theory of circulation explain the endless appearances and disappearances, but do not explain the transformation of the elements. But the mysterious interchanging theory is different. *Chou I* has no logical explanation about this phenomenon (that the Yang element changes into the Yin element or the Yin element transforms into the Yang element), and treated this phenomenon as a Kuei Shen's (鬼神) act.[54] Kuei Shen can be considered as a mysterious something that humans cannot count or measure. On the other hand, Kuei Shen can be defined as a Yin-Yang relationship—Kuei as a Yin and Shen as a Yang—and can be analyzed as a logical relationship of Yin-Yang.[55]

In the explanation of the Chou Hsi Theory (朱子推橫圖卦畫之原), Kang Chuen Bong said, "Yin numbers and Yang numbers have the particular nature of Pien (變) and Hua (化). If Yin becomes extreme and it transforms, Yang becomes extreme and it changes. If Yang changes its place, Yin follows the neighboring friend." This explanation means that Yin can change by itself and Yang can transform by itself. There are many theories and explanations about the Yang Pien Yin Hua (Yang changes to Yin and Yin changes to Yang), but the logical and systematic explanation of the theory is only in the divination with divining sticks and calculation of the result (Hsi Fa, 筮法). When one draws the divining sticks three times, the sum of the sticks should be one of 25, 21, 17, or 13. When these numbers are subtracted from 49, the remaining numbers are 24, 28, 32, or 36. When these numbers are divided by 4, the result should be 6, 7, 8, or 9. If the resulting number is 6, it is old Yin in which Yin is extreme (老陰), number 7 is young Yang (少陽), number 8 is young Yin (小陰), number 9 is old Yang (老陽) in which Yang is extreme. Young Yin and Young Yang are unchangeable, but old Yin and old Yang represent an extreme situation, so they change. When this phenomenon is analyzed by the shape of odd or even numbers, old Yang is three odd numbers and old Yin is three even numbers. Young Yang is one odd number and two even numbers; young Yin is one even number and two odd numbers. Because pure even numbers (three even numbers) and pure odd numbers (three odd numbers) are an extreme situation—they can change to Yin or transform to Yang—they can make change. But young Yang or Young Yin cannot change, so they cannot make change.[56]

Chou I treats change as a very important matter and the changes of the lines completes the trigram. The change (易) explains the timely condition and is used as a way to predict future changes. Of course, these kinds of changes transcend human ability, so they were treated as mysterious happenings and attributed to Kuei Shen's (鬼神) play. The thing which makes the lines of the trigram change is called a flying god (飛神) and the thing before change is called a latent god (伏神).

Figure 3-12
Post-Heaven Order of the Eight Trigrams
(後天八卦次序圖)

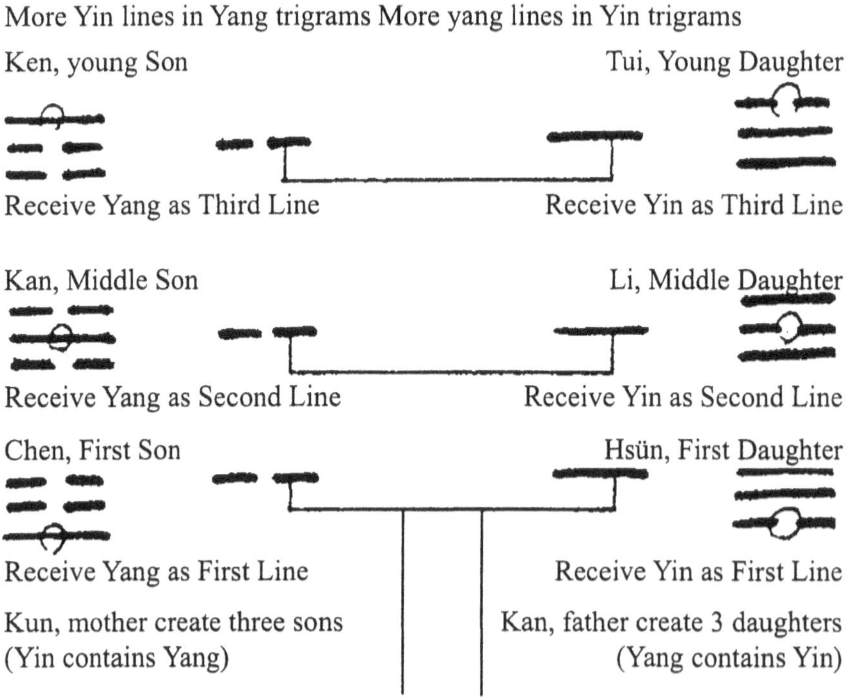

More Yin lines in Yang trigrams   More yang lines in Yin trigrams

Ken, young Son   Tui, Young Daughter

Receive Yang as Third Line   Receive Yin as Third Line

Kan, Middle Son   Li, Middle Daughter

Receive Yang as Second Line   Receive Yin as Second Line

Chen, First Son   Hsün, First Daughter

Receive Yang as First Line   Receive Yin as First Line

Kun, mother create three sons   Kan, father create 3 daughters
(Yin contains Yang)   (Yang contains Yin)

Material: 退溪學報 第七輯, p.131

Figure 3-13
The Order of Eight Trigrams of King Wen
(文王八卦次序圖)

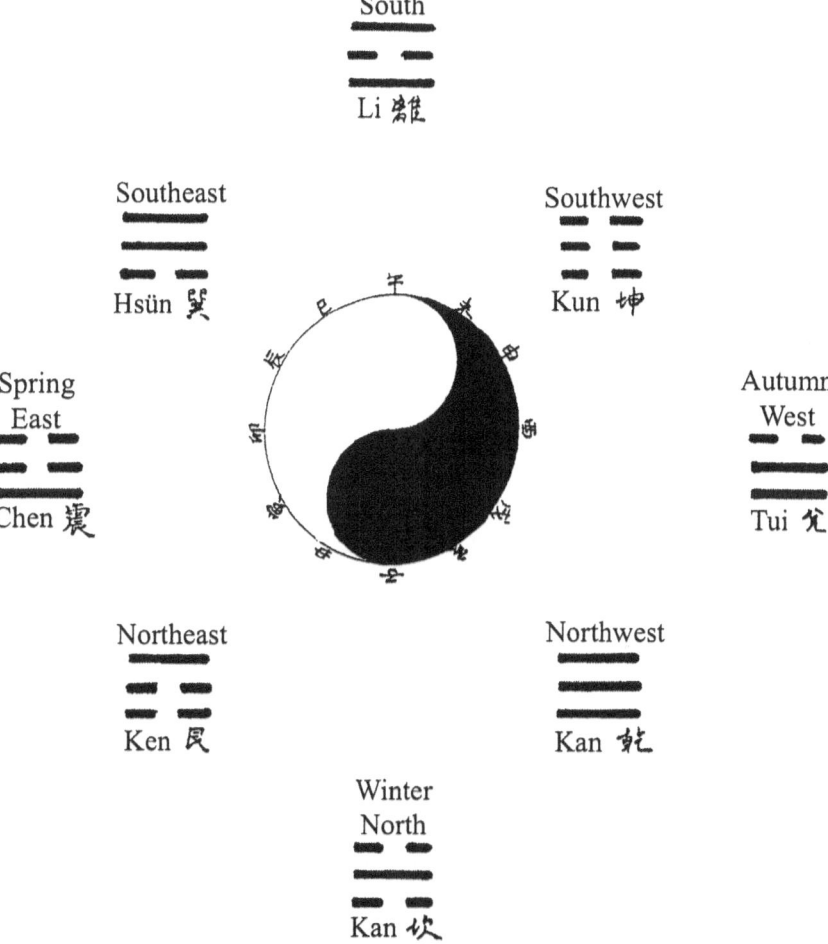

Material: 退溪學報 第七輯, p.135

The change of the Yin-Yang can be explained through the Figure of the Order of the Eight Trigrams of King Wen (文王八卦次序圖) or the Figure of the Function of the Eight Trigrams (八卦用事圖).

Toegae said, "The Yang is inside the Yin and the Yin is inside the Yang in only four positions. These four positions are Tzu (子), Wu (午), Mao (卯), and Yu (酉). Wu is the extreme position of the Yang, so it is the time the Yin starts to grow. Tzu is the extreme position of the Yin, so it is the time when the Yang starts to grow. In principle, the Yang is inside the Yin and the Yin is inside the Yang at these two positions. Mao is the east direction. The Yang is at the middle position in the east, so it is not extreme. If the Yang is not extreme, the Yin should be in the middle of that position. Yu is west. The Yin is at the middle position in the west, so it is not extreme. If the Yin is not extreme, the Yang should be in the middle. In general, there is no Yin or Yang that exists far apart from other between the heaven and the earth. So get the meaning of one extreme and one beginning, and take the meaning that because it is not extreme, both the Yin and the Yang exist together in the middle. Therefore, nothing is impossible."[57] As in the above description, Toegae praised the Figure of the Function of the Eight Trigrams of King Wen.

There are three important meanings in his explanation. First, the theory that the Yin is inside the Yang and the Yang is inside the Yin can be expressed in two ways. The Figure of the Order of the Eight Trigrams shows that two Yang lines and one Yin line are in the Yin trigram, and that two Yin lines and one Yang line are in the Yang trigram, and explained the reason why Yin and Yang combine. The Figure of the Function of the Eight Trigrams shows that the Yin and the Yang stay together at the same time and in the same place during the alternate creation of the Yin-Yang. Second, in the Figure of the Order of the Eight Trigrams, a Yang trigram (乾 , ☰) takes one Yin line and changes to a Yin trigram (巽 , ☴) and a Yin trigram (坤 , ☷) takes one Yang line and changes to a Yang trigram (震 , ☳). The Figure of the Function of the Eight Trigrams shows that when Yang is extreme it is then that the Yin starts to grow and when the Yin is extreme Yang starts to grow through the Figure of the Alternate Creation of the Yin Yang. Third, the Figure of the Function of the Eight Trigrams shows the orderly creation of five elements—the wood element (木),— the fire element (火),— the soil element (土),—the metal element (金),—and the water element (水). But if the Figure of the Alternate Creation of the Yin-Yang inside the Figure of the Function of the Eight Trigrams is not a shape of (☯) but is the shape of (☯), the figure would show much more clearly that Yin is inside Yang and Yang is inside Yin. And if the figure of the Alternate Creation of the Yin-Yang (陰陽生盛交替圖) is connected to not only the Figure of the Direction of the Eight Trigrams of King Wen (文王八卦方位圖) but also to the Figure of the Direction of the Eight Trigrams of Fui (伏羲八卦方位圖), the creation of Yin-Yang, and of the seasons, would coincide completely (see Figure 3-14).

According to this figure, Tzu (子) time is mid-winter and is a pure Yin period. This time is described as the earth (地,坤,☷) and is when the Yang element starts to grow. Chou (丑) time and Yin (寅) time, when Yang is growing but Yin overpowers Yang, is expressed as the thunder (雷,震,☳) and the season is early spring. Mao (卯) time, when Yang pushes out Yin but when their powers are similar, is expressed as the fire (火,離,☲) and the season is spring. Chen (辰) time and Ssu (巳) time, when Yang grows and overpowers Yin, is expressed as the pond (澤,兌,☱) and the season is early summer. Wu (午) time, when Yang pushes out Yin completely and is a pure Yang period, is expressed as the heaven (天,乾 ☰); the season is mid-summer and Yin starts to grow. Wei (未) time and Shen (申) time, when Yin pushes out Yang but Yang overpowers Yin, is expressed as the wind (風,巽,☴) and the season is early autumn. Yu (酉) time, when Yin pushes out Yang but both powers are similar, is expressed as the water (水,坎,☵) and the season is autumn. Hsü (戌) time and Hai (亥) time, when Yin pushes out Yang but Yin overpowers Yang, is expressed as the mountain (山,艮,☶) and the season is early winter. Time turns into a pure Yin period after all this, and the seasons circulate endlessly. When Fui's Figure of the Direction of the Eight Trigrams and the Figure of the Alternate Creation of Yin-Yang are combined together, the creational function of the Yin-Yang, the shapes of eight trigrams, the changes of the seasons, and the phenomena of Yang Pien Yin Hua (陽變陰化), Yang Chung Han Yin (陽中含陰), and Yin Chung Han Yang (陰中含陽) are described fairly well.

The theory of Yang Pien Yin Hua has been analyzed and summarized. These theories can generalized as two conclusions: "The Yin and the Yang are created alternately. This process is inevitable and the creation of the Yin-Yang causes the change. The unification of Yin and Yang creates the things that appear with the Yang nature or the Yin nature or

Figure 3-14
The Direction of the Eight Trigrams of Fui and Alternate Creation of Yin Yang
伏羲八卦方位圖와 陰陽生盛交替圖

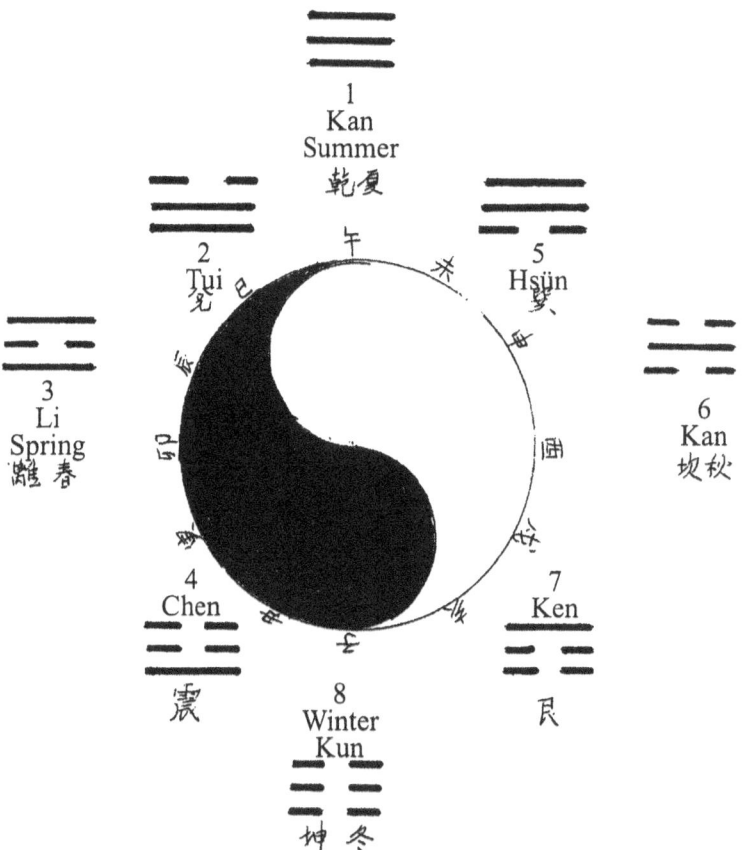

the neutral nature, and these created things contain both the Yang and Yin elements. The theory of Yang Pien Yin Hua seems like a different expression of the next two theories, rather than mysterious happenings. The first theory is the alternate creation of Yin-Yang and circulation. The second theory is Yang Pien Yin Ho (陽變陰合)—that when the Yang element moves, the Yin element follows Yang and unites with it."

Cycling Order

Another theory of change is the theory of circulation and repetition. The definition of change adopted the great premise that nothing is fixed and unchangeable and that nothing is the same permanently—that the maxim of nature is endless change and continuous cycling and repetition. This means that all things are changing according to the natural law of cycling and repetition.

The explanation of the third line of the Tai hexagram (泰卦) said, "There is no plain thing that is not slope, there is no going without returning. Even if you are in trouble, just do the right thing and don't worry, only sincerity will say."[58] And in the explanation of the Ku hexagram (蠱卦), Sim Jong Chuel said, "The disorder must be recovered, that is the law of nature."[59] These two explanations define the phenomenon of circulation and repetition as natural. The circulation and repetition means that the same events repeat periodically. Things periodically grow and perish or are growing continuously by repeating the cycle of growth and rest.

The most basic theory of circulation concerning change is in the theory of Tai Chi, the explanation of which says: "Tai Chi moves and creates the Yang, when it moves extremely it becomes static and static Tai Chi creates Yin. When it becomes static extremely, it starts to move again. The alternation of one movement period and one static period divide the Yang and the Yin, and they oppose and confront each other."[60] So the function of the Tai Chi is a repeating creation of Yin-Yang. This kind of cycling is found in the ancient Tai Chi Tu, and the creation of the five elements is also a theory of circulation and repetition. In the Figure of Co-creation of Ho Tu (河圖相生圖), the water element creates the wood element, the wood element creates the fire element, the fire element creates the soil element, the soil element creates the metal element, and the metal element creates the water element. And in the Figure of Co-challenge of Lo Shu (洛書相克圖), the water element checks the fire element, the fire element checks the metal element, the metal element checks the wood element, the wood element checks the soil element, and the soil element checks the water element. This process of creation is a cycling process.

The circulation theory of change coincides with the movement of the celestial sphere. According to the explanation of Tai Chi Tu, "When the Yang element changes, the Yin element follows the Yang and unifies to the Yang (陽變陰合) and creates the water element, the fire element, the wood element, the metal element, and the soil element. Five elements spread in an orderly way, so the four seasons are moving."[61]

Therefore, Tai Chi Tu explains that the unification of Yin and Yang creates the five elements and the movement of the two and five elements creates the four seasons.

Chapter 6 of the *Upper Chi Tzu Chuan* described, "The change and the communication accord with the four seasons and the meanings of Yin Yang coincide with the sun and moon."[62] Chapter 5 of the *Lower Chi Tzu Chuan* explained, "The sun is down, the moon is up; the moon is down, the sun is up; and the sun and the moon push each other and create the light. The coldness goes, the hotness comes; the hotness goes and the coldness comes; the coldness and the hotness push each other and complete a whole year. Going is bending and coming is stretching; the bending and the stretching react with each other and create the benefit."[63]

Tuan Tzu of the Feng hexagram (豐卦的彖辭) says, "If the sun stands at midday, it begins to incline; when the moon is full it begins to wane. The fullness and the emptiness of heaven and earth is a waxing and waning depending on time—how different in the case of man or gods!"[64] The Kan hexagram (乾卦) also explains the 6th line: "When it waxes in full, it does not stay long."[65]

All of these explanations attempted to accord the celestial movement (such as day or month) with the circulation of Yin-Yang and the five elements. In other words, the movement of Yin-Yang and the five elements causes the celestial movement and the celestial movement causes the change of day and night, seasons, and years—and the change of human life, too.

Several periodic times have been introduced. The periodic times of the Yin-Yang and the Wu Hang movement can be short or long and the change also can be small or large. Chou I uses seven steps of periodic time. The explanation of the Fu hexagram (復卦) states, "Repeat the way, return on the seventh day—this is the course of heaven."[66] Because hexagrams are constructed with six lines, if one line changes a day or a month, it will return to its original state in the seventh day or month—this circulation is a seven-step cycling. The most basic periodic times are day, month, and year. The day is a rotation time of the earth, the month is the revolution time of the moon, and the year is the revolution time of the earth. Four years periodic time (a leap year) or twelve years periodic time are used sometimes.

The most particular periodic time is the 129,600 years of the creation of the heaven and the earth of Hiao Kang Chieh (邵康節). He defined an hour as 30 minutes and a day as 12 hours, so a day is 360 minutes, a month is 10,800 minutes and a year is 129,600 minutes. And he insisted upon the minute unit-periodic times. If we count a year as a periodic interval, we would have a little change every 30 minutes (1 hour), a middle change every 360 minutes (1 day), a great change every 10,800 minutes (1 month), and a great great change every 129,600 minutes (1 year). If we use a year unit-periodic time—a little change of one Shih (世) every 30 years, a middle change of one Yun (運) every 360 years, a great change of one Hui (會) every 10,800 years, and a new creation of the heaven and the earth every 129,600 years—then that is a completion of the Wu Hang movement of the celestial body.[67]

Han Dong Suek followed Kim Il Bu's theory that came from Hsiao Kang Chieh's theory. He defined the great change of one Hui (10,800 years) as a period of repeat-of-axis change of the earth, which inclined 23.7 degrees. According to him, the axis of the earth repeats the coming and going at the North Pole every 5,400 years. During pre-heaven's 5,400 years, the Over-Yang phenomenon (3 heaven, 2 earth) induces the dispersion of Tai Chi, so it creates severe conflict and contradiction. But from AD 2000, when post-heaven's 5,400 years began, there will be a harmonious unification movement.[68]

The periodic period of Hsiao Kang Chieh will remain as a hypothesis until the axis of the earth changes in reality, but the periodic time of day, month, and year are real periodic intervals and these cycles lead the change of nature. The movement of the celestial body changes not only environments, but also human beings. The environmental change causes physical and psychological change in humans. So as a change of nature circulates, a change of humans also circulates. Therefore, the circulation and repetition is a kind of change by itself and it causes change.

The theories of circulation in Chou I have been analyzed. When we generalize all of these theories we find that the theory of creation, the theory of Yang Pien Yin Hua, and the theory of circulation are the same theories. The process of creation is a process of circulation, the alternate creation of Yin-Yang is a circulating process, and the function of Yang Pien Yin Hua is a kind of creation. The dispersion of Tai Chi (creation of Yin-Yang and the five elements) or the unification of Yin-Yang and Wu Hang are changing functions. Creation, growth, and extinction mean change by themselves—they are both causes and processes of change. It remains a question if the goal of creation is an increase of production or a continuous circulation. No matter what the answer is, the sure thing is that all of these happenings are part of change.

Harmonious Unification (和合)

The word *Ho Ho* (和合) means harmonious unification which is a combination of two virtues—the harmony and the union. *Chou I* praises the unification of the Yin element and the Yang element because it means creation, which is a goal of the Tai Chi movement. Especially, *Chou I* emphasizes the harmonious unification among them.

The importance of the harmonious unification was demonstrated very well in the comparison of the contrary hexagrams. Typical instances of the contrary hexagrams are the Tai and Pi hexagrams (地天泰卦,天地否卦), the Chien and Sung hexagrams (地山謙卦,天水訟卦), and the Hsien and Kuei hexagrams (澤山咸卦,火澤睽卦). The Tai hexagram means harmonious union while the Pi hexagram means dispersion. Tuan Tzu and Hsiang Chuan of the Tai hexagram (泰卦的彖辭,象傳) expressed, "Intercourse of the heaven and the earth is Tai. The heaven and the earth intercourse with each other, so all things communicate with each other. The upside and downside unify, since both share a same goal."[69]

The heaven (☰) is at a lower place and the earth (☷) is at a higher place. This hexagram looks like it is upside-down, but it is not. The Yang element is light, so it goes upward; the Yin element is heavy, so it goes downward. Therefore, they meet in the middle and unify and communicate with each other—everything goes well. On the other hand, the Pi hexagram shows an opposite meaning. As the Tuan Tzu and Hsiang Chuan of the Pi hexagram (否卦的彖辭,象傳) describe, "The failure of intercourse between the heaven and earth is Pi. If the heaven and the earth fail to intercourse, all things fail to communicate with each other and there is no nation under the heaven."[70] This hexagram means that heaven and earth fail to intercourse. The upper trigram, Kan (☰), is light, so it goes upward, and the lower trigram, Kun (☷), is heavy, so it goes downward. Because they go astray and fail to intercourse, all things fail to grow.

The Chien and Sung hexagrams are similar cases. The Chien hexagram carries out the harmonious unification, but the Sung hexagram shows discord. The Chien (謙) means modesty. Tuan Tzu of the Chien hexagram described this hexagram. "Tuan said that the reason why modesty is going through is that the heaven's way goes downward and lights up brightly, the earth's way goes upward from the low place; the heaven's way subtracts from fullness and adds to modesty, earth's way changes the fullness and makes it humble. The god deducts the fullness and makes modesty felicitous, and human's way hates the fullness and likes the modesty. The modesty is high and shinny, even though it is low it cannot be crossed over; therefore, it is a final goal of a king."

In explanation: "The element of the strength of heaven (陽氣) comes down and raises all things, so it lights up brightly. The earth stays at the low place so the element of strength of earth (陰氣) goes upward and responds to the heaven's movement. The heaven's way subtracts from the fullness and adds to the places that are lacking. As if reducing the high mountains and filling up the deep valley, the earth's way changes the full things and adds to the places that are lacking. The god's way brings misfortune to the rich and gives fortune to the humble man; the human's way hates arrogance and prefers modesty. When a modest man occupies the high position, he brightens; even though he is in the low position, he is not in contempt."[71]

The Chien hexagram unifies high and low harmoniously, and equalizes them, but the Sung hexagram shows a discordant shape between high and low. Hsiang Chuan of the Sung hexagram explains. "Sung means that the heaven mismatches with water, a suit is somewhat sincere but is blocked in some times." In the Sung hexagram, the element of strength of heaven goes upward and the water runs downward, so they go astray and cause a suit. The upper trigram Kan (乾, ☰) is sturdy and the lower trigram Kan (坎, ☵) is dangerous. A high-classed man suppresses a lower-classed man with strong authority and the lower-classed man covets the upper position, so it causes a suit. One is compelled to fight by the other; if one persists to fight until the end, both sides will suffer as a result.[72]

Comparison of the Tai and Pi hexagrams shows the difference between the unification and the dispersion, but comparison of the Chien and Sung hexagrams shows the difference between the harmony and the discord.

The comparison between the Hsien hexagram (澤山咸) and the Kuei hexagram (火澤睽) shows the difference between the male-female harmony and the female-female discord. The Hsien hexagram shows the sympathy between the male and the female. Tuan Tzu of the Hsien hexagram described the Hsien. "According to Tuan Tzu, Hsien is feeling. The mildness goes upward and the sturdiness goes downward, two elements of strength react to each other and feel the pleasure of each other. Man lowers down toward woman, so everything goes well. If one does the right thing, he will benefit; if one obtains a woman, he will be fortunate. The heaven and the earth interreact with each other and create all things. A saint inspires humans, so the world becomes harmonious. If one understands sympathy, he will understand the feeling of all things in the world."[73] In other words, when a man takes a lower posture and inspires a woman, and when the woman accepts the man's sincerity and responds to him pleasantly, they intercourse harmoniously.

On the other hand, Kuei represents discord. Hsiang Chuan of the Kuei hexagram explains the Kuei. "In the Kuei hexagram, fire is on the upper side and pond water is on the lower side. According to Tuan, fire goes upward and pond water goes downward. Two women live together but their wills are different."[74] Kuei means that the upper trigram and the lower trigram miss each other on the road and fail to unify. Two women obstruct each other, regard each other with jealousy, and all things are unsuccessful because of the disharmony.

The above comparisons demonstrate that harmonious unification is better than antagonistic dispersion. Also expressed is that the goal of nature is a creation through the unification of the Yin element and Yang element and that the best shape of unification is a harmonious unification.

A few models of Yin-Yang unification can be defined and introduced. The first model is harmonious unification as described previously. As described in the Tai, Hsien, and Chien hexagrams, Yin and Yang unify harmoniously without any resistance because the two elements face each other and share their will to unify. The pure hexa-grams (純卦) and the Tung Jên hexagram (同人卦) show the unified action because two trigrams have the same natures or same goals to achieve.

Another model of unification is the Sui-Tsui model (隨萃型). In the Sui-Tsui model, one side follows the other side unilaterally. The Chun hexagram (屯卦) shows the unification after they have overcome the obstruction; the Shih Ho hexagram (噬嗑卦) achieves unification in a noisy, conflicting process.

The pure hexagrams are constructed with two of the same trigrams. The Kan hexagram (乾卦), Kun hexagram (坤卦), Kan hexagram (坎卦), Li hexagram (離卦), Chên hexagram (震卦), Kên hexagram (艮卦), Sün hexagram (巽卦), and Tui hexagram (兌卦) all belong to this model. These pure hexagrams show unified actions, all the time, without any objections. Even though it is not a pure hexagram, the Tung Jên hexagram (同人卦) maintains the union because the two trigrams have the same natures. According to the Tung Jên hexagram, "The heaven and the fire go together so it is Tung Jên; the king classifies the things by race."[75] In the upper trigram, Kan is the Yang trigram and heaven, while the lower trigram, Li, is the Yin trigram and fire, so both trigrams have natures to go up and meet the people impartially. The pure hexagram and the Tung Jên hexagram show that comrades who share the same view go together—it is not the unification of Yin and Yang, but it is a harmonious and non-conflicting union. However, this union is conditional, presuming the leader will maintain the middle position and maintain rightness and fair play.

The Sui hexagram (隨卦) achieves unification by having one side follow the other unilaterally, without condition. The Sui hexagram described, "The sturdiness goes down toward the mildness, be pleased by moving. When first son (震，長男) is moving, young girl (兌，少女) accepts him pleasantly."[76] When one side follows the other side pleasantly, they can unify harmoniously because they do not resist one another.

The reversed hexagram of the Sui hexagram, the Kuei Mei hexagram (歸妹卦), also can unify harmoniously. Even though the positions of the lines are not correct positions and the structure is not ideal, it can carry out the unification of Yin and Yang just like the Sui hexagram.

The Tsui hexagram (萃卦) is a shape showing if a king implements virtuous policies, people gather together. Tsui explains, "Tsui is gathering, obeying pleasantly without objection; the sturdiness takes the middle position, so people gather."[77] The upper trigram, Tui (兌), is pleased, and the lower trigram, Kun (坤), is mild and gathers pleasantly. In this hexagram, if the line of the king's position maintains the right posture and governs the country virtuously, people will happily follow the king. Therefore, this hexagram has important political meaning in that it is a harmonious unification of the civilian and the government.

Though not ideal models of unification, Tung Jên, Sui, Kuei Mei, and Tsui do carry out the harmonious unification. In the Chun and Shih Ho hexagram, Yin and Yang unify through a difficult process. The Chun hexagram (屯卦) has a hard shape (or structure) to unify because of obstacles; it moves in dangerous conditions and unifies only after going overcoming obstacles. Tuan Tzu of the Chun hexagram described, "The strong and the weak move for the first time, creating the danger; the movement in danger makes everything go fairly well."[78] In the Chun hexagram, the upper trigram Kan (坎, ☵) is dangerous and the lower trigram Chên (震, ☳) is moving. The Chun hexagram is in a dangerous time when the sturdiness and the mildness meet for the first time and create something. Therefore, in this situation one should go over the danger dauntlessly in order to unify.

The Shih Ho hexagram (噬嗑卦) is a model of conflicting unification. The Hsiang Chuan of the Shih Ho hexagram explains. "Something is inside the mouth, so it is an unification through the mastication—everything can go well after chewing and unifying. The sturdiness and the mildness stand separately and are lightened by movement, the thunder and the lightening combine and brighten things. The mildness takes the middle position and goes upward, so it is good to treat the justice and the punishment."[79] When something is inside the mouth, the upper teeth and the lower teeth rub each other and unify through friction. After eating, through mastication, everything goes through. Even though the Chun and Shi Ho hexagrams do not create harmonious unification because of the difficult process, they carry out creation through the unification of the Yin and Yang elements.

Above, we found that Chou I praised harmony and unification and expressed dislike of conflict and dispersion. But Chou I occasionally treats conquest as a just thing. There are such records in the Chien (謙), Li (離), Kuai (夬), and Ko (革) hexagrams.

Hsiao Tzu (爻辭) of the fifth line of the Chien hexagram said, "The fifth line goes together with his neighbors without haughtiness of wealth; it is beneficial to conquer the enemy. Hsiang said, 'Telling that it is beneficial to conquer means a conquest of the disobedience.'"[80] When a king governs the people with virtue, people obey him because they are inspired, not because of the reward. According to Chien, even though the king possesses the Chien and is virtuous, if people do not obey him, then conquering them is just.

In the explanation of the sixth line of the Li hexagram, Hsiao Tzu said, "If the sixth line (king) goes forward and conquers, it will be beautiful (beneficial). Because this honor can be acquired by conquest of the leader of the enemy, if they are not same kind, there will be no fault. According to Hsiang, going forward and conquering is a straightening of the nation. Cutting the leader of enemy with great virtue is not a fault."[81]

Sim, Jong Chuel explained the Kuai hexagram (夬卦). "The sixth line, the Yin line, is top of the five Yang lines. One weak line above the several strong lines means that one private interest is above several public interests. This is itself an unforgivable crime. Even though there might be some dangers, the Yang must drive out the Yin; thus, the king's way becomes brighter."[82]

Finally, the Ko hexagram means revolution. Ko is a disharmonious hexagram that can go well only after change. Tuan Tzu of the Ko hexagram (革卦的象辭) described the Ko hexagram as follows: "The water and the fire kill each other, two women live together but they cannot share the same goals (the Ko hexagram is the reversed hexagram of the Kuei hexagram). The explanation that the belief comes on Chi day (己日) means that the belief comes after reform. The civilization let people submit, so opens widely. Correction and reform are proper solutions, so there is no regret. The change of the heaven and the earth makes four seasons. King Tang (湯王) and King Wu (武王) set up the revolution and follow heaven's way and response to people—oh the time of revolution is great!"

The upper trigram of the Ko hexagram is the pond water (兌 , ☱) and the lower trigram is the fire (離 , ☲).[83] The water goes downward and the fire goes upward, so they collide against each other. The youngest daughter and middle daughter live together but their goals are different, so this hexagram is in a situation that should be changed. The water beats the fire when the water is prosperous but the fire beats the water when the fire is prosperous. Revolution is in accord with the laws of nature only when the reform is just and proper. Therefore, King Tang of the Yin dynasty and King Wu of the Chou dynasty followed the order of heaven and responded to the people when they reformed their governments.

So the Chien, Li, Kuai, and Ko hexagrams justify conquests which are types of disputes. Especially in the Ko hexagram, conflict and struggle are inevitable in the process of reform because the Ko hexagram is in a condition that must change.

Life and the death, unification or dispersion—all are causes of change and are unreturnable phenomena of the natural order, but the time of creation and unification is defined as a good time. Whether the unification is difficult (like the Chun or Shi Ho hexagrams) or harmonious (like the Tai or Hsien hexagrams), no matter what model of unification is used, unification is a kind of process of creation and is an achievement of the goals of heaven and earth. Therefore, unification is a great virtue of nature and is good. But Chou I recommended harmonious unification. The environmental conditions and the structure of the hexagrams are important factors in harmonious unification (like in the Tai-Hsien model), as is human will to consciously pursue such unification. When Yang approaches Yin with a humble posture—like in the Chien or Hsien hexagrams—harmonious unification is a possible outcome. When a king or leaders follow the harmonious middle line, people can trust them and follow them of their own accord. If a king or leaders are impartial (公平無私) and behave in the righteous middle line (中正), people will obey and can unify harmoniously. In the Chien and Hsien hexagrams, the Yang approaches the Yin with a lower posture. So the public officials (大人) approach to the private workers (小人) with modesty and a man approaches a woman with a humble manner. The Chien subtracts from richness and adds to poorness, reduces from highness and adds to lowness. Therefore, a woman is influenced by a man and private workers are influenced by public workers—and they unify harmoniously.

In the Tai, Hsien, and Chien models, it is simple to explain the technique of the harmonious union. However, it is not so simple in other models. The Tung Jên hexagram (同人卦) shows the great general union of six lines because the fifth line (king's position) takes an impartial public line (大道). Here, Ta Tao (大道) means a cardinal principle (王道) or universalism. The *Book of Great Learning* (大學章句), the *Book of Moderation* (中庸章句), and the *Book of Change* (周易) explain the Ta Tao in detail.

The *Book of Great Learning* said, "The way of great learning is lightening the bright virtues, is renewing the people by inspiration, is maintaining the extreme virtue." The *Book of Moderation* said, "Heaven gives the nature (性), lightening of the nature is Tao (道), teaching the lightened nature is Chiao (教)." The *Book of Change* said, "King is a man who performs the four virtues. So Kan (乾) is Yuan Heng Li Chen (元亨利貞), Ta Jên (大人) goes together with the virtue of nature (heaven and earth)." The virtue that is mentioned in the *Book of Great*

Learning, the nature mentioned in the *Book of Moderation*, and the four virtues mentioned in the *Book of Change* are all the same virtues. They are the humanity (仁), the righteousness (義), the courtesy (禮), and the wisdom (智).[84]

The Confucius school understood that these four virtues came from the four elements of strength—the wood (木), the fire (火), the metal (金), and the water (水)—by one out from one. So they defined these natures as the four original natures granted by heaven.

According to the *Book of the Great Learning*, the goal of study and training is the awakening of the original nature and implementing that nature. Therefore, as the book said, the goal of learning is lightening the bright nature, renewing the people with brightened virtue, and maintaining the condition of extreme virtue. The *Book of Moderation* also mentioned the heaven-given natures and the *Book of Change* also described the kingship as executing the four virtues.

The king (君子), or Ta Jen (大人), is the public leader who possesses the bright virtue and performs the four original natures. He stays away from his personal desires completely and behaves only according to the four original natures which heaven granted. When a king or leader behaves like this saint, all the people will obey him and he can accomplish the great union.

The appearance of the saint who possesses the purely impartial virtue not only creates harmonious union, but also changes human society. According to the *Book of Great Learning*, when a saint carries out the Ching Chu Chih Tao (絜矩之道), then all the family members are inspired and all the people in the world are inspired, and the world becomes peaceful. Therefore, man starts to train by himself, inspires all the people, and carries out political change.

The next measure of harmonious unification in the *Book of Change* is Chung Cheng (中正). Chung Cheng is a major thought in the *Book of Change*. Thirty-three hexagrams mention the middle line in explanation of the 64 hexagrams. The words, "medium," "mid-way," "mean," "moderation," etc., are used very often. The book explains that the middle line is a great foundation, one in which everything goes well and succeeds in almost all situations. The importance of the middle line can be generalized as: "When one follows the middle line, he can accomplish almost all things. Even if one is in trouble, he can solve the problem easily in the middle line. Therefore, moderation is a virtue by itself and is a right thing by itself."[85]

The second line of the Kan hexagram explained: "The second line takes the exact middle line—talk trustfully, behave sincerely, abolish the evil way and respect sincerity, do not praise oneself about doing a good deed, broaden virtue and inspire people. Seeing Ta Jên (大人) is beneficial, so it is a king's virtue (君子之德)." According to the Kan hexagram, the middle line is a king's way (君子之道).

The meanings of the middle line were edited in a separate book, the *Book of Moderation*. This book is one of four basic books of the Confucian school. It has been known that, Tzu Ssu (子思), grandson of Confucius, generalized Confucius' teachings, and that Chu Hsi (朱熹) interpreted the book, but the author of this book has yet to be determined. Because the meanings of the words "medium," "mid-line," "mean," and "moderation," which were described in the *Book of Change*, are the same as in the *Book of Moderation*, and because the content of the two books are of Confucian thought, it is possible that the writers of the two books were the same person. Or perhaps the similarities are because the scholar who both collected and interpreted the scattered ancient books was Chu Hsi (朱熹). In any event, the questions concerning the authors of these books is a subject for future study.

The concept of the middle line has no true character, it is just middle as it is. Chapter 4 of the *Book of Moderation* said, "I know why the doctrine (道) is not performed—because a wise man knows too much and a foolish man knows too little. I know why the doctrine is not bright—because the intellectuals know too much and the silly men fall far behind." This paragraph explains the middle line as not too much and not too little (無過不及).

Chapter 6 of the *Book of Moderation* said, "Oh, Shun (舜) is a wise man! He likes to ask, pleasures to watch even trivial things, hides the evil and praises the good, determines both ends and picks up the middle line, and applies it to people." That chapter also introduced the technique of the performance of the middle line by using King Shun's example. According to this explanation, the moderation does not have particular character—it can change both in time and place. Therefore, King Shun inspected the public opinion, determined both ends, and applied the mean to the people.[86]

This concept of the middle line includes not only the concept of the mean but also that of the balance of the mind. The maintenance of the balance of the mind means attaining a spiritual state of perfect selflessness or controlling the mind consciously or freely. Chapter 1 of the *Book of Moderation* begins, "Heaven orders man to respect the bright nature (天命之謂性)." It explains the Chung Ho (中和) thusly: "The feelings, the gladness, the anger, the grief, the pleasure are not expressed in the condition of the middle line. Even though these feelings are expressed, they stop at the middle in the condition of harmony. The middle line is a most basic foundation of the nature and the harmony is omnipotent doctrine of the nature (喜怒哀樂之未發謂之中發而皆中節謂之和致中和天地位焉萬物育焉)."[87] This is a theory of mental training which follows the principle of creation reflecting Yin-Yang and Wu Hang and Tai Chi. The explanation also complicates matters. The theory can be summarized as follows. When Tai Chi creates Yin-Yang and Yin-Yang creates the five elements—the wood, the fire, the metal, the water, the soil—each element gives man one nature. They are the humanity (仁), the righteousness (義), the courtesy (禮), the wisdom (智), and the trust (信). These natures are called heaven-given natures (天性) or original natures (本性). On the other hand, the gladness (喜), the anger (怒), the grief (哀), and the pleasure (樂) are passions.

According to the traditional Confucian school, these passions are different from the original natures. Because the heaven-given original natures are pure goodness, they lead humans toward good deeds without consideration of over- or under-expression. But because human passions are mixed with impure elements, it is good in only controllable conditions and can be bad in overly-expressed conditions. Therefore, when human passions (the gladness, the anger, the grief, and the pleasure) are not expressed, man behaves according to only the original natures. This situation is called the middle line condition (中). On the other hand, even when human passions are expressed, and if they are under control, the situation is defined as the harmonious condition (和). So the state of moderation is the mental condition that maintains the middle line situation or the harmonious condition.

According to Toegae, the original virtues, which are purely good, are fighting with passions which can be bad in certain conditions—all inside the human mind. He developed the mind control technique (敬) and introduced the way to perform Ching (敬) consciously.[88]

When we generalize the theories of the middle line, the following conclusion is possible. Because the middle line takes a mean of a certain period, it assures fairness (or impartiality); so the middle line can carry out the great union (大同團結), it also inspires humans and changes human society and political fields.

Cheng (正) and Chen (貞) mean "right," "just," or "straight." Right behavior or just action can make for a harmonious unification, just as can the performance of the middle line. The explanation of the 64 hexagrams and their lines used the phrases "doing right is beneficial (利貞)," "righteousness brings good luck (貞吉)," and "straight (貞)" many times (in fact, 135 times). The word "Chen (貞)" is used in the Yüan Heng Li Chen (元亨利貞) in the explanation of the Kan hexagram.

Yüan (元) means "top," "first," or "great," Hêng (亨) means "be clear," "go well," or "go through;" Li (利) means "profitable" or "beneficial;" and Chen (貞) means "right" or "straight." According to Wen Yen (文言), Yüan means "top of virtue," Hêng means "meeting of beauty," Li means "unity of righteousness," and Chen means "core of thing." A king learns righteousness by experience so he is sufficient to be a leader. The gathering of beauty is enough to accord with courtesy, the using things is coincide with right reason, and righteousness is sufficient to be the main stream of the things.

The original writing of *Chou I* (周易本義) described the Yüan as spring (春), humanity (仁), virtue (善); the Heng as summer (夏), courtesy (禮), beauty (美); the Li as autumn (秋), righteousness (義), maturity (成熟); and the Chen as winter (冬), wisdom (智), fruit (結實).[89]

Chapter 2 of the *Upper Chi Tzu Chuan* explained the Chi (吉). "A saint makes the trigrams (八卦) and explains them after he examines the Kua, and judges the good or ill luck. The sturdiness and the mildness bring the change by pushing each other, so good or bad (吉凶) means 'take or lose.'" Chapter 1 of the *Lower Chi Tzu Chuan* also said that the good or ill luck means "right thing win."[90] In other words, Chi (吉) is taking and Hsiung (凶) is losing; Chen Chi (貞吉) means that doing the right thing is advantageous.

When we generalize the above analysis of Li (利), Chen (貞), Chi (吉), we arrive at the following that Li Chen (利貞) means "The right thing is just;" and that Chen Chi (貞吉) means "Doing the right thing is beneficial and the right thing wins."

Chou I described the Chen as: "Even though you are in trouble, if you do right thing it will be beneficial," or "king should follow the right way, so he will be beneficial." In *Chou I*, straight means right, and righteousness has a few meanings. The first meaning of righteousness is naturalism. Behavior that is in accordance with the law of nature is defined as a right behavior. Chapter 1 of *Chi Tzu Chuan* said, "Chi Hsiung (吉凶) means that righteousness wins. The doctrine of the heaven and the earth is right observation, the doctrine of the sun and the moon is right light, the movement of the universe has only one right way." According to *Chi Tzu Chuan*, behaviors that are in accordance with the natural order are right actions because natural change is correct change.

The second meaning of righteousness is as the middle line. In the Confucian school, the middle line is a right line and a just line. As in the previous explanation, because the middle line is impartial and controls human passions, it can create great harmony and union.

The last method of harmonious unification is that of virtuous politics or of a generous government (德治). Tê (德) means a virtue or goodness. Tê is Jen (仁). Jen is one of the four basic virtues (仁，義，禮，智); in fact, it is the top virtue of the four. The *Book of Moderation* and the *Book of Mencius* explained about the Tê Hang (德行) and the theory of Jen virtue was analyzed in the diagram of Jen Shou (仁說圖) in the Ten Diagrams of Saint Learning (聖學十圖).

Chapter 20 of the *Book of Moderation* said, "Politics belong to man; one can train his body with doctrine (道) and learn the doctrine from the Jen virtue."[91] This means that if a king carries out the generous virtues, people will follow the king's model and become inspired. In the chapter on politics in *The Analects of Confucius*, Confucius compared the generous king to the North Star. "As the North Star takes its place and all other stars follow it, if a king is virtuous and governs the people with generosity, people will perceive the disgrace and will go the right way. But if a king introduces the law and governs people with punishment, people will try to escape only law network." So he insisted that the best policy is to inspire people with virtuous governing.[92]

Mencius also insisted upon virtuous governing—"one action, one inspiration (一致一化)." *The Book Three of Mencius* explained virtuous governing. "We call the man a supreme ruler who governs the people with force and feigns being a virtuous man, and we call the man a king who governs the people with virtuous ways. When the governor suppresses the people with force, people will obey only in appearance because they are not strong enough; but if a governor governs the people with virtue, people will obey him whole-heartedly, so all the people of the country will obey him."[93]

So it is very similar to the virtue of modesty of the Chien hexa-gram (謙卦). The meaning of the virtue (德) includes the four basic virtues—the humanity (仁), the righteousness (義), the courtesy (禮), and the wisdom (智)—and also includes the modesty (謙), the selfless impartiality (大道), the middle line (中庸), and the mean and just (中正).

Chu Tzu (朱子) explained the Jen Shuo Tu (仁說圖). "Jen (仁) is a thought that the heaven and the earth create all things, so the great virtue of creation becomes a Jen thought. Before the thought occurs, it contains all four virtues (仁, 義, 禮, 智), but only Jen (仁) covers all other three virtues. When the thought occurs, all four virtues are expressed, but only Jen (仁, 惻隱) penetrates through all four."[94] So Chu Tzu emphasized on the Jen." Therefore, Tê (德) contains several virtues, and the virtuous behavior and the virtuous governing inspires others and achieves the great harmony and the great union.

The harmonious unification (和合) is an important value claim and is an important theory of change. Even though both unification and dispersion are theories of change, harmonious unification is a core value of creation. Therefore, the research focused on the development of the environment to unify, and on methods to unify harmoniously. The methods of harmonious unification are the modesty (謙), the selfless impartiality (大道), the middle line (中庸), and the mean and justice (中正). These techniques of harmonious unification are enhanced by virtuous governing (德治), and one can accomplish the greatest harmony and greatest union by using these techniques.

Balance (均衡)

The balance of the Yin element and the Yang elements is treated as a favorable condition. When Yin and Yang unify and create something, if the Yin element and the Yang element are balanced, the created result is bigger than the result in unbalanced cases. The concept of balance and the concept of stability are contrary concepts to the concept of change. According to *Chou I*, the theory of change is a continuously changing process of the dispersion and the unification of the Yin and Yang elements. Therefore, the concept of balance should be a timely concept. *Chou I* insists upon not only the price of balance but also the value of the Fu Yan

I Yin (扶陽抑陰). Because the concept of Fu Yang I Yin has a contrary meaning of balance, the Fu Yang I Yin is introduced before the balance is analyzed.

Chou I insisted that both Yin and Yang are necessary elements for creation and change and that inclining toward one side is not a desirable phenomenon. But in the relationship between the two elements, *Chou I* expressed clearly that Yang is prior to Yin.

In the explanation of Chi Seng Po Yang Yueh Hun (既生魄陽曰魂) of the book of *Chi Meng Chuan I* (啟蒙傳疑), Toegae said, "Single Yang can not start creation and solitary Yin can not complete creation. If Po (魄) is there, Hun (魂) is prepared, and if Hun is there, Po should follow it."[95] This means that neither Yin or Yang can accomplish anything by itself. In the explanation of the Sui hexagram (隨卦), Sim, Jong Chuel insisted, "Yin cannot stay alone, must follow Yang. That is the principle of the unification of Yin-Yang."[96]

The explanation of the Kun hexagram (坤卦) said, "If Yin goes in advance she will lose her way, but if Yin goes in behind she will take advantage. As a sixth line, dragons fight in the fields, so blood is black and yellow. According to Hsiang, fighting in the fields means the lack of virtue. Yin should follow Yang initially, but if Yin becomes prosperous and Yin's power is equally matched with Yang, Yin fights with Yang. In this situation both sides will be hurt and will bleed. If Yin becomes vigorous, it is difficult to maintain a normal condition."[97]

The original writing of *Chou I* also said, "Even though Yin possess the beauty, but if Yin engages in king's affairs Yin will fail. If Yin is similar to Yang, Yin fights with Yang certainly because Yin confuses the situation that there is no Yang around."[98] In the above description, *Chou I* insisted that Yang is a leader and Yin is a follower, Yang is the head and Yin is tail, Yang is the front and Yin is the rear.

The Yang—Prior—Thought stands because Yang is thought to be a cause of creation or the origin of life. In the explanation of the figure of (蔡氏四十九耆虛一體數圖), Toegae said, "The disappearance and the diminution (消息) means quality rather than quantity; in general, the Yin-Yang have a principle of support and suppression. When Yang changes to Yin this change means diminution rather than growth, when Yin changes to Yang this change means growth rather than diminution.

"The Yang grows from the bottom in the Chên trigram (☳) and the Yin grows from the bottom in the Sun trigram (☴). Even though the principle of the growth is the same, the growth of Yang is defined as growth and the growth of Yin is defined as diminution. This kind of particular interpretation that supports the Yang and suppresses the Yin is called the Principle of the Support Yang and the Suppress Yin (扶陽抑陰). Therefore, the phenomenon that old Yang change to young Yin is called disappearance (消) and the phenomenon that old Yin change to young Yang is called growth (息)."[99]

In the explanation of the function of the five elements, Han Dong Suek also gave a similar explanation. He defined the wood and fire elements as Yang elements and the metal and water elements as Yin elements. According to him, the Yang element makes the dissolution and the growth, while the Yin element makes the unification and the suspension. The dissolution and the growth, the unification and suspension—all of these functions are important, but when we observe the perennial plants we can find that they grow during the spring, the summer, and the autumn at different speeds, and stop growing during the winter season, and that they repeat this process for several years. We also find that the Yang element is a motive power of growth. Therefore, living beings who want growth and an increase of production must treat the Yang element as noble and Yin element as ignoble.

The principles of the Support Yang and Suppress Yin (扶陽抑陰) and the Thought of Noble Yang and Ignoble Yin (大貴小賤思想) are expressed well in the comparison of the opposite hexagrams. They are the Kou (天風姤卦) and Fu hexagrams (地雷復卦), the Tun (天山遯卦) and Lin hexagrams (地澤臨卦), the Pi (天地否卦) and Tai hexagrams (地天泰卦), the Kuan (風地觀卦) and Ta Chuang hexagrams (雷天大壯卦), and the Po (山地剝卦) and Kuai hexagrams (澤天夬卦).

In the Kuo hexagram, the Yin element is growing from the bottom but its power is not strong enough to threaten Yang; in the Fu hexagram Yang is growing but its power is not strong enough to threaten Yin. Kuo is defined as a declining time and Fu is defined as a beginning growth time. Therefore, Toegae interpreted the Fu hexagram this way: "Decayed time is gone and active time is coming."[100]

In the Tun and Lin hexagrams, the growth of the Yin and Yang elements is much more active so the expression is also stronger. Tun recommended avoidance because Yin is growing and Yang is declining. One can do well by escaping in the Tun situation. On the other hand, the Lin is explained as: "The sturdiness is growing so everything goes well and it is the heaven's way."[101] Especially, Toegae warned about the Tun hexagram. "It is a shape where two Yin lines are growing and pressing Yang hard. If you have this hexagram you have to know that an enemy who harbors suspicion and resentment is seeking the opportunity for revenge. It is the shape of the chased weak Yang by the vigorous Yin, and if you face your enemy, you will be defeated surely. So the best strategy is escaping or avoiding him."[102]

The most extreme example is the comparison of the Pi hexagram and the Tai hexagram. The explanation of the Tai hexagram said, "In Tai, small affairs are going and big affairs are coming, so it is lucky and goes very well. The heaven and the earth intercourse with each other, so everything goes through. The uppers and the lowers unite and share their goals. The king is inside and the civilian is outside, so the public interests are growing and the private interests are diminishing." The growing Yang in the Tai hexagram is described as good luck; however, everything is blocked in the Pi hexagram. The explanation of the Pi hexagram said, "Pi is not a human way; even though the king does the right thing, it is not beneficial. Big affairs are going and small affairs are coming. Tuan said that Pi is not a human way, even if the king does the right thing, it is not advantageous. Big affairs are going and small affairs are coming. The heaven and the earth failed to intercourse, so all things are blocked. The uppers and the lowers fail to unify, so there is no nation. The king is outside and the civilian is inside, so the private interests are growing and the public interests are diminishing." An annotation explains: "The king escapes and hides and private men will become exasperated as if they have their own world."[103]

Toegae also said that everything goes well in the Tai hexagram and all things are blocked in the Pi hexagram.[104] All of these explanations express the great difference between the time in which Yang is growing from the time in which Yin is growing.

The difference between the Po and Kuai hexagrams is great, too. The explanation of the Po hexagram said, "In the Po hexagram, Yin invades (erodes) Yang and changes the sturdiness to mildness so the action stops. When a private person persecutes a public person, if you continue it will not be beneficial." On the other hand, the explanation of Kuai hexagram said, "The shape where one mild line is on the top of five strong lines means that one private person is above five public persons. The behavior of this private person is itself unforgivable. The punishment of this person may bring danger, but the king's virtue will be brightened more."[105]

In the above explanation, the difference of the action where Yang pushes out Yin to the one where Yin pushes out Yang is great. Even *Chou I* treated both Yin and Yang as important elements, but it expressed clearly that Yang is noble and Yin is ignoble. This is the Principle of the Support Yang and Suppress Yin (扶陽抑陰).

Even though *Chou I* prefers the Yang over the Yin, it also prefers the balanced unification of Yin-Yang rather than leaning toward one or the other. These kinds of value claims are well expressed in the Ta Kuo hexagram (澤風大過卦) and the Hsiao Kuo hexagram (雷山小過卦). In the Ta Kuo hexagram, four Yang lines are in the middle position, while one Yin line is on the top and the other Yin line is at the bottom. The Yang is excessive in this hexagram. The explanation of the Ta Kuo hexagram said, "A girder is bent in Ta Kuo." According to Tuan, the Yang is excessive in Ta Kuo, and the reason a girder bends is that the basis and the end are weak. This means that if Yang is excessive, the Yin and the Yang are unbalanced, so the girder is bent. This hexagram is the shape that the wood plants sunken in the pond water. Especially, the explanation of the third line and the sixth line expressed the excessive Yang phenomenon. "Third line is a bent girder so it is ugly. According to Hsiang, ugliness of a bent girder has no way to straighten itself. The sixth line crosses the water excessively, so it sank under the water up to the forehead, but it is not a blameful thing."[106]

Toegae also explained the Ta Kuo phenomenon using similar logic. "Ta Kuo means excess. The pond water overflows and becomes a flood in the Tui trigram (兌 , ☱), while the Sun trigram (巽 , ☴) means the wind or the wood. So this hexagram shows the shape of trees that are troubled by the flood. Therefore, if you have this hexagram, you must perceive that you are in anguish and toil. Because of excessive expansion of business and excessively heavy responsibility, you are in agony and you can accomplish nothing, so you have to find the thing that is fit for you."[107]

The excessive Yin phenomenon is shown in the Hsiao Kuo hexagram (小過卦). Hsiao Kuo is the shape where two Yin lines are on the top and two Yin lines are at the bottom, with four Yin lines surrounding the two middle Yang lines. So the Yin lines are excessive in this hexagram. The explanation of the Hsiao Kuo hexagram said, "Hsiao Kuo goes through. If one does the right thing he will benefit, it is possible to do small affairs. If the word of a flying bird goes up it will be wrong, but if the word comes down it will be right and will have great luck."[108]

Hsiao Kuo explained that the excessive Yin is not a favorable phenomenon. Toegae also insisted that excessive Yin is not good thing. "Hsiao Kuo is an excessive condition where two Yang lines get in between four Yin lines—do not act freely in this hexagram. Because of the vigorous private interest, the king's measure is not brightened. Therefore, when you have this hexagram you must presume that you will be placed in an awkward position by the trick of a small man (private interest)."[109]

The Po hexagram (剝卦) and the Kuai hexagram (夬卦) also show that the unbalanced structure of Yin-Yang is not a favorable condition. In the Po hexagram, five Yin lines are pushing out one Yang line. Of course, its structure is not favorable. In the Kuai hexagram, five Yang lines are pushing out one Yin line. According to the Principle of Support Yang and Suppress Yin, the Kuai structure should be a favorable phenomenon. But the explanation of Kuai hexagram is not favorable: "Inform to the court (government) and cry loudly, so it is a dangerous condition. Informing the village and mobilizing troops is not beneficial. If one has a place to go it is a good thing."[110] Toegae also lectured that excessive Yang is not a good phenomenon. "Kuai means decision. The spirit of five Yang lines stretch upward, so it is the shape where the lower class assaults the higher class. Because the shape of this hexagram brings dangerous affairs, one must expect a lawsuit or intimidation and blackmail."[111]

The above analysis can be generalized by stating that *Chou I* insisted upon the preference of Yang in the interrelation between Yin and Yang, but prefers the balance of Yin and Yang—and balanced unification, especially—and treats the phenomenon which inclines toward one side as a unfavorable one.

Stability

A science of change praises the change and attaches itself to the importance and the processes of change, but it does not disregard the importance of the stability. *Chou I* introduced two concepts of stability. The first is the theory of unchange (不易理論), which states: The change has the principle of change, so the principle of change should not change.

The second concept is found in the characteristics of Yin-Yang. The elements of Yin and Yang have different natures, so each element should do the right action at the right position in order for the whole system to be stable. This is the theory of stability (安定理論). The theory of unchange means a natural order. The principle of the creation of Yin-Yang and the five elements and all things is an unchangeable principle; the principle of the cycling order is an unchangeable principle. Therefore, all the changes should occur upon the changing order. If the seasonal change and the creational change do not occur according to certain principles, there will be no normal movement of Yin-Yang and no normal creation of all things. So the theory of unchange insists that change is acceptable, but that the process of change and the method of change should be stable.

The theory of stability is well-demonstrated in the Hêng hexagram (雷風恒卦) and the Chia Jên hexagram (風火家人卦). The explanation of the Hêng hexagram said, "According to Tuan Tzu, Hêng is eternity. The sturdiness goes upward and the mildness comes downward, the thunder and the wind move together, the sturdiness and the mildness respond to each other. Because the virtue of Hêng lasts long, Hêng goes through well, has no fault, and is beneficial, if it does the right thing. The virtue of the heaven and the earth is permanent. If one goes somewhere it will be beneficial—this means that if there is an end there should be a beginning. The sun and the moon provide light for a long time upon heaven's principle; four seasons cycle for a long period. A saint continues his virtue for a long time, so it enlightens the world. If one sees eternity, he will see the feelings of all things in the world. According to Hsiang, the thunder and the wind are permanent, so the king stands and does not change direction." In its explanation, the upper trigram is the first son (震,長男) and the lower trigram is the first daughter (巽,長女). The male is in a higher place while the female is in a lower place; a woman lowers her posture to a man. This is the normal relationship between a husband and a wife—if their relationship is to be long-lasting.[112]

In the Hsien hexagram (咸卦), a woman comes down from a higher place and a man goes up from a lower place, so they meet in the middle and achieve the intercourse between the Yin and Yang. On the other hand, in the relationship between a married couple, the wife should lower her posture to the husband in order for their relationship to last. To put it another way, the husband has his function and duty and the wife has her function and duty. When each do their own duties well, the relationship will continue for a long time; this principle should not change for stable human lives.

The Yin lines and Yang lines construct the hexagram and each line has a responding line. When responding lines are constructed with a Yin line and a Yang line, it is a proper structure and is stable. In the hexagram, the first and fourth lines, second and fifth lines, and third and sixth lines respond to each other. When corresponding lines are constructed with the Yin and Yang lines, this structure is better than the response among either Yin lines or Yang lines. When the first, third, and fifth lines are Yang lines, and the second, fourth, and sixth lines are Yin lines, this structure is a proper structure. When the second line is Yin and the fifth line is Yang, it is the best structure of all and is called the Chung Chêng (中正) structure.

This kind of structure is well-described in the Chia Jên hexagram (風火家人卦) and the Chi Chi hexagram (水火既濟卦) shows the best structure. The explanation of Chia Jên hexagram said, "In Chia Jên, woman is inside at the right position and man is outside at the right position. The possession of the right positions of man and woman is a great virtue of the heaven and earth. There is a stern king in Chia Jên, they are parents. When the father acts as a father, the husband acts as a husband, and the wife acts as a wife, the family order will run true. When families are correctly ordered, the world becomes stable."[113]

The first line of Chia Jên is the son, the second is the woman, the third is the second son, the fourth is the woman, the fifth is the first son, and the sixth is the father. Because the second line stays inside the Chung Chêng position of Yin and the fifth line stays outside the Chung Chêng position of Yang, and because all the family members perform their roles in their proper positions, the family maintains a stable condition. The Chia Jên hexagram demonstrates that human society can accomplish its social goals and maintain its function under stable conditions when the components of human society—such as family, company, or government—do their duties under the established order.

Just as in the natural order, human society also should be constructed so that each member does their duty at the suitable position. When the structure and the principle of function are stable, human society can accomplish its goals and maintain stability for a long time.

Problems of the Theory of Change

Theories in *Chou I* are logical, in general, and they are common theories which are well-versed in all subjects, but there are a few problems. Because the theory of change begins with metaphysical theories (such as Tai Chi, Yin Yang, and Wu Hang), it is impossible to verify them scientifically. Many interpretations of following generations have been found that they do not fit reality or are not in accordance with modern science. The impossibility of verifying *Chou I* theories may come from the limitation of human knowledge—lack of verification does not necessarily equal falsehood. Interpretations which do not fit modern science may come from a false interpretation of *Chou I*; again, that does not mean the theory of change is false.

Beyond these questions, three basic problems are found in the theory of change. They are the contradiction between change and stability or balance, the contradiction between human will and naturalism, and the contradiction between birth control and population increase. These problems arise from the contradictions among *Chou I*'s value claims.

To begin with, *Chou I* asserts both the natural order and the human will. As a principle of living, *Chou I* insists upon obedience to nature (順理) in several places. The obedience to nature without any objection is naturalism and Hao Jan thought (浩然思想).

Chou I explained the fifth line of the Kan hexagram as follows: "In general, the great man (大人) accords with the virtue of heaven and earth, accords with the lightness of the sun and moon, accords with the order of the four seasons, and accords with the good or ill luck of Kuei Shen (鬼神). When he acts in advance of heaven, heaven does not act against him. When he follows heaven, he follows the time of heaven. Even heaven does not act against him, much less Kuei Shen or man!"[114]

In this context, the "great man" means a saint. Sainthood is a final goal achieved by studying and training. The saint understands the natural order fluently and behaves according to nature. When that accordance is maximized, he achieves complete union with heaven (天人合一). Even though nature changes often, there are unchangeable rules of change. Because a human is a being of nature, if he learns the laws of the nature and trains himself, he can enter into a state of complete union with nature. Therefore, according to Sim Jong Chuel, "Even though man has the ability to exploit his own future and can change his fate under the given condition, he cannot go against nature. Don't be haughty about your richness and nobleness, and don't worry about your poorness—there is only a way of up and down."[115]

Chapter 4 of the *Upper Chi Tzu Chuan* lectured, "The theory of change coincides with the heaven and the earth, it unites with the virtue of the heaven and the earth, so look up to the heaven's rule and look through the earth's rule. Therefore, one knows the causes of death. Questioning and knowing about the beginning and then looking to the end, allows one to understand the principle of life and death. The essential element (精氣) becomes the body and the wandering spirit (遊魂) is changing, so understand the shape and the feeling of Kuei Shen (鬼神). So one coincides with the heaven and earth, nothing is against each other; the wisdom spreads to the whole world, the virtue saves the world. If one does not go excessively, even though one goes sideways, he will not spill over, he admits heaven pleasantly and understands heaven's way. Therefore, he does not worry about anything, is as calm as the soil, is sincere in benevolence. So he can love with. He takes the harmony of the heaven and the earth as a standard, does not go excessively. All things are achieved heartily, so there is no surplus, and the principle of the day and night are known thoroughly. Therefore, god has no direction and change has no shape."[116]

Chapter 6 of the *Upper Chi Tzu Chuan* lectured, "The size and extent accord with the heaven and the earth, the changing and passing through accord with four seasons, the meaning of Yin-Yang accords with the sun and moon, the simplicity of change theory accord with extreme virtue." [117]

The lectures of *Chi Tzu Chuan* can be generalized into two conclusions. First, the theory of change analyzed the principles of nature, so if one knows the theories of change. Then one will know life and death—one can even understand the action of Kuei Shen. So it is said that nature and human beings are created and become extinct according to the same principles.

Second, the saint who has thorough knowledge of change understands the natural order (the laws of nature). So he does not worry about and can love all mankind and all the things in the world through humanity (仁, 德). Furthermore, he can inspire entire populations to follow the natural order; he can save the world and mankind who keep fighting for their own desires and are drowning in agony.

The Tuan Tzu of the Yü hexagram (雷地豫卦的彖辭) said, "The sturdiness responds and acts by the will in the Yü hexagram. The Yü hexagram moves according to the law of nature. Even the heaven and earth is like this; moreover, it is also the case with setting up a king and with the deployment of troops. The heaven and earth move by the principle, so the sun and moon move on time. Four seasons do not go wrong with nature, saints act according to the natural order. Criminal law and the punishment is enlightened, so people obey him. Oh, the timely meaning of the Yü hexagram is great."[118] This means that politics can be enforced properly and that people obey when politics accord with the laws of nature.

The above examples of Wen Yen (文言), Chi Tzu Chuan (繫辭傳), and Tuan Tzu of Yü (豫卦的彖辭) are typical examples of Hao Jan thought (浩然思想). According to its proponents, human beings are created and change according to the laws of nature. Therefore, human beings should live according to nature. It is a truism that if one goes against nature he will be defeated and if one lives according to the laws of nature he will benefit and he can achieve his mission. They also insisted that if a man confronts all things and affairs in sincerity, problems will be solved easily. But if one seeks good fortune with an unfaithful mind, he will instead bring disaster. So man should imitate the truthful model of the heaven's mind and carry out it in real life.[119, 120]

This logic is a fatalism—that man should accommodate to nature. If we follow this logic, human ability to cultivate nature and the human will to reconstruct nature are not allowed, and thus man loses the right of autonomy to decide his own fate. The contradiction between man's autonomy and fatalism is a basic problem with the theory of change.

The second problem lies in the conflict between change and stability or balance. The balance in question is the balance between the Yin element and the Yang element, and the stability is the stable relationship between the two. But because nature changes continuously, it cannot maintain the state of balance or remain in a stable situation all the time. In order to sustain the balanced or stable situation, the state should not change. But nature never permits permanent balance or permanent stability. The theory of change is a something about the change. In order to create a thing, and in order to achieve the great virtue of nature, nature must change. The basic problem is that if it changes it will be unstable and unbalanced.

The third problem lies in the conflict between the theory of cycling order and the Principle of the Support Yang and Suppress Yin (扶陽抑陰). Even though the theory of change recognizes the equal function of the Yin and the Yang, it demonstrates the value claim clearly in that it treats the Yang as the noble one and the Yin as the ignoble one; it praises the public way or king's way and disregards the private way. Therefore, the theory of change intends for growth and an increase in production, and avoids the degeneration and reduction of output. Analysis of this subject needs to take into consideration the cycling theory of Han Dong Suek. According to Kim Il Bu, Han Dong Suek's teacher, because the change theory of Confucius is a theory of the pre-heaven period, it gave superiority to the Yang. Because he thought the Confucius theory to be incorrect, he attempted to fix it. According to him, it becomes a post-heaven period (5400-year period after AD 2000) and human physiology and psychology changes in order to fit in the period of the unification rather than the dispersion, so the Yin-leading period comes.[121] In this theory, the Yang element is vigorous in the pre-heaven period, so Yang leads to the increasing production in this period and Yin leads unification in the post-heaven period in which the Yin element is vigorous. It is questionable whether or not birth control and the decrease in population are symptoms of the post-heaven period. If there is a cycling period that is an alternating period of a Yang-leading period and a Yin-leading period, this theory does not coincide with Confucian theory. Of course, modern human beings have both the physiology and the psychology to fit with increasing production. Therefore, Ta Tao (大道) is the right way to them, and it is normal that public man follows the Ta Tao or public way (大道). In any event, the conflict between the theory of change which leads to an increase of population and the theory of change which leads to a decrease of population is a basic problem of *Chou I*. It remains a problem for future study.

Notes

1. Kang, Chuen Bong,
   姜天奉, "啓蒙傳疑硏究" 退溪學報 第三輯, 서울 : 退溪學硏究院, 1974. p.81. 上同, 第五輯. p.178. 沈鍾哲, 周易, 서울, 大韓曆法硏究所, 1979. pp.9.

2. Kang, Chuen Bong, ibid. p. 80.
   姜天奉, "啓蒙傳疑硏究" 退溪學報 第三輯, p.80, 여기에는 "易大傳河出圖, 洛出書, 聖人則之", "孔安國云, 河圖者, 伏羲氏 王天下, 龍馬出河, 遂則其文, 始畵八卦, 洛書者, 禹治水時, 靈龜負文, 而列於背, 有數陳之, 九疇是也"를 해석하였음.

3. Lee, Sang Eun,
   李相殷, 聖學十圖譯解, 서울 : 退溪學硏究院, 1982. pp.47~52, 退溪의 生涯와 學問, 서울 : 瑞文堂. 1978. pp.181~238.

4. 繫辭上傳, 第十一章에는 "是故 易有太極 是生兩儀 兩儀生四象 四象生八卦", "이런고로 易에 太極이 있으니 이에서 兩儀를 生하고 兩儀는 四象을 生하고 四象이 八卦를 生하니"라고 설명하여 易의 本體가 太極임을 명확히 하고 있다. 그 해설에서 하나가 둘이 됨이 自然理致이고 易은 陰陽의 變化라고 하여 여기서 말한 兩儀가 陰陽임을 시사했다.
   繫辭下傳, 第六章에도 "子曰 乾坤其易之門邪 乾陽物也, 坤陰物也, 陰陽合德 而剛柔有體" "子 가라사대 乾과 坤이 易의 門인져, 乾은 陽物이오, 坤은 陰物이니 陰陽의 德이 合하여 剛柔의 體가 있음이라"고 하였다.
   金赫濟, 原本集註 周易, 明文堂, 서울 : 1987. p.381, p.406. 여기서 말하는 兩儀란 乾과 坤을 말하며 이것이 陽과 陰을 뜻한. 繫辭傳에는 陰陽의 特性과 作用에 관한 여러 說明이 있지만 대부분의 경우 乾坤으로 표현하고 社會의 變易을 설명할때는 剛柔로 對立시킴.

5. Han, Dong Suek, 韓東錫, 宇宙變化의 原理, 서울 : 행림출판사, 1985. p.28

6. Kim, Hyuck Jae, Kang, Chuen Bong,
   金赫濟, 上同. p. 4. 姜天奉, 上同. 第七輯. p.112.
   韓東錫, 上同. p.284.

7. Kim, Hyuck Jae,
   金赫濟, 上同. p.353. 天尊地卑하니 乾坤이 定矣오 卑高以陳하니 貴賤이 位矣오 動靜有常하니 剛柔斷矣오 方以類聚코 物以群分하니 吉凶이 生矣오 在天成象코 在地成形하니 變化見矣라. 是故로 剛柔相摩하며 八卦相盪하야 鼓之以雷霆하며 潤之以風雨하며 日月運行하며 一寒一暑하야 乾道成男하고 坤道成女하니 乾知大始오 坤作成物이라. 同. p.356. 剛柔相推하야 而生變化하니. 여기서 天과 乾은 陽을 표시한 것이며, 地 · 坤은 陰을 표시한 것이다. 이외에도 陰陽作用에 대해서 繫辭傳은 많은 講論을 하고 있다. 繫辭上傳 第六章, 第十一章, 第十二章 繫辭下傳, 第一章, 第六章, 第十二章 참조.

8. Lee, Sang Eun,
   李相殷, 聖學十圖譯解, 上同. p.15. "無極而太極, 太極動而生陽, 動極而靜, 靜而生陰, 靜極復動, 一動一靜, 互爲其根, 分陰分陽, 兩儀立焉, 陽變陰合, 而生水火木金土, 五氣順布, 四時行焉, 五行一陰陽也, 陰陽一太極也, 太極本無極也".

9. Lee, Sang Eun, ibid. 李相殷, 上同. pp.16~17.
10. Lee, Sang Eun,
李相殷, 上同, "五行之生也, 各一其性. 無極之眞, 二五之精, 妙合而凝. 乾道成男, 坤道成女, 二氣交感, 萬物化生, 萬物生生, 而變化無窮焉"
11. Han, Dong Suek, 韓東錫, 宇宙變化의 原理, 행림출판사, 1985. p.292.
12. Kim, Hyuck Jae, 金赫濟, ibid. p. 364. There are many descriptions of the characteristics of Yin and Yang. In chapter 5 of Upper Chi. Tzu Chuan said, "Kan moves straightly and Kan's spirit is pure, so accomplishment is great. Kun closes in a quiet time and opens in a moving time, so accomplishment is great." Chapter 11 of the same book says, "Kan opens the door and Kun closes the door." According to chapter 12 of the Lower Chi, Tzu Chuan states, "Kan is extremely sturdy, so it performs the virtue easily and understands the difficulty easily. Kun is extremely docile, so it performs the virtue simply and understands the blockage." p. 425. According to Shuo Kua Chuan, "Kan is a horse, Kun is a cow, Kan is the head, Kun is the abdomen. Kan is the father, Kun is the mother; Kan is heaven, a circle, a king, a father, a gem, a gold, a coldness, a ice, a great red, a horses, a tree fruit. Kun is an earth, a mother, a draper, a pot, elegance, equality, a cow, a large wagon, a culture, a mass, a bottle, a black."
13. Kim, Hyuck Jae, ibid. p. 4, p. 22.
Sim, Jong Chuel, ibid. p. 24. p. 36.
金赫濟, 上同. p.4, p.22. 沈鐘哲, 上同. p.24. p.36.
"象曰大哉라 乾元이여 萬物이 資始하나니 乃統天이로다. 雲行雨施하야 品物이 流形하나니라. 大明終始하면 六位時成하나니 時乘六龍하야 以御天하나니라. 乾道가 變化에 各正性命하나니 保合大和하야 乃利貞하나니라. 首出庶物에 萬國이 咸寧하나니라.", "象曰至哉라 坤元이여 萬物이 資生하나니 乃順承天이니 坤厚載物이 德合无疆하며 含弘光大하야 品物이 咸亨하나니라. 牝馬는 地流이니 行地无疆하며 柔順利貞이 君子攸行이라 先하면 迷하야 失道하고 後하면 順하야 得常하리니 西南得朋은 乃與類行이오 東北喪朋은 乃終有慶하리니 安定之吉이 應地无疆이니라."
14. Kim, Hyuck Jae, ibid. p. 308, p. 385. (乾坤其易之縕耶 乾坤成列而易 立乎其中矣 乾坤毀則无以見易 不可見則乾坤或幾乎息矣)
15. Lee, Sang Eun, ibid. p. 15. "五行一陰陽也, 陰陽一太極也"
16. Kim, Hyuck Jae, ibid. p. 3 p. 5.
17. Kim, Hyuck Jae,
金赫濟, 上同. p.397. "陽卦는 多陰하고 陰卦는 多陽하니 其故는 何也오, 陽卦는 奇요 陰卦는 偶일지라 其德行은 何也오, 陽은 一君而二民이니 君者之道也이오 陰은 二君而一民이니 小人之道也이라"
18. Lee, Hwang, p. 119. According to Toegae's explanation, "Change is Yang Pien Yin Hua of numbering in the creation. When number one changes into the water element (水氣), number six completes this. When number two changes into the fire element (火氣), number seven completes this. When number three changes

into the wood element (木氣), number eight completes this. When number four changes into the metal element (金氣), number nine completes this. When number five changes into the soil element (土氣), number ten completes this." This means that odd numbers of Yang and even numbers of Yin unify with each other and create all things. The trigrams express the Yin character or the Yang character but the Yin lines and the Yang lines are harmonized inside. Two Yang lines and one Yin line construct the Yin trigram, and two Yin lines and one Yang line construct the Yang trigram. Therefore the Yin trigram has more Yang lines and the Yang trigram has more Yin lines. So Yin becomes Yang's mother and Yang becomes Yin's father. The Yang Pien Yin Hua is shown in the theory of alternate creation of the Yin-Yang and in the Fei Fu Ting Wei (飛伏定位 and 互藏宅變).

19. Kim, Hyuck Jae, ibid. p. 383.

金赫濟, 上同. 繫辭上 第十一章, p.383. 是故로 天生神物이어늘 聖人則之하며 天地變化어늘 聖人이 效之하며 天垂象하여 見吉凶이어늘 聖人이 象之하며 河出圖하며 洛出書어늘 聖人이 則之하니 易有四象은 所以示也오 繫辭焉은 所以告也오 定之以吉凶은 所以斷也라. 同 第九章 p.371. 天一地二天三地四天五地六天七地八天九地十이니 天數가 五이오 地數가 五이니 五位相得하며 而各有合하니 天數가 二十有五이오 地數가 三十이라 凡天地之數가 五十有五이니 此가 所以成變化하며 而行鬼神也이라 …

20. Kang, Chuen Bong, ibid. p. 80.

姜天奉, "啓蒙傳疑研究〔1〕", 退溪學報 第三輯, 上同, p.80, 易大傳河出圖, 洛出書, 聖人則之. 孔安國云, 河圖者, 伏羲氏 王天下, 龍馬出河, 遂則其文, 始畵八卦, 洛書者, 禹治水時, 靈龜負文, 而列於背, 有數, 陳之, 九疇是也.

21. Kang, Chuen Bong, ibid. p. 83.

姜天奉, 上同. pp.83. "天以一生水 而地以六成之, 地以二生火 而天以七成之, 天以三生木 而地以八成之, 地以四生金 而天以九成之, 天以五生土 而地以十成之".

22. Han Dong Suek, ibid. p. 86.
23. Kang Chuen Bong, Han Dong Suek,

姜天奉, 退溪學報 第三輯, pp.89~70. 退溪는 여기서 張晏의 説을 해석함. 韓東錫, 上同. pp.53~73. "木爲仁 仁者生, 生者圓, 故行生泰之權, 原始東方陽散泄, 而生風, 風乃生木, 其性屬少陽, 陽中含陰, 故體騰上, 而質柔軟".

24. 上同. "火爲禮, 禮者齊, 齊者平, 故行炎陽之令, 主成齊之權, 原始南方陽極, 而生熱, 乃生火, 性屬太陽, 雖陽物竪在其內, 故其體內暗, 質燉烈".

25. 上同. 金爲義, 義者成, 成者方, 故行收斂之令, 主肅殺之權, 原始西方陰止收, 而生燥, 燥乃生金, 其性屬小陰, 陰中含陽, 故體光明, 質堅剛.

26. Kang Chuen Bong, ibid.

上同. "夫水者爲智, 智者謀, 謀者重, 故行嚴凝之令, 主殺物之權, 原始北方陰極而生寒, 寒乃生水, 性屬太陰 雖陰物, 陽含於內, 故其體內明, 質沈潛".

27. Kang Chuen Bong, ibid.
上同, "土爲信, 信者誠, 誠者直, 故處五行之中宮, 行負載之令, 主養育之權, 原始中央陰陽相交, 而生濕, 濕乃生土, 性無常性, 視四時所乘, 喜相濟得所, 其體包水火木金之四物, 故蒙虛實, 而質持散合."

28. Han, Dong Suek, ibid.

29. Kang Chuen Bong, (退溪學報, 第三輯), ibid. p. 108.
Han Dong Suek, ibid, (相火章) Six elements means that once fire is added to the five elements, a proper noun is attached to them as Wind wood, King fire, Co-fire, Dry metal, Moist soil, and Cold water. Each element is allotted sixty days, so January and February are Wind wood, March and April are King fire, May and June are Co-fire, July and August are Dry metal, September and October are Moist soil, and November and December are Cold water. According to Han Dong Suek, the declination of the axis of the earth causes this phenomenon.

30. Kim, Hyuck Jae,
金赫濟, 上同, p.422, 退溪學報 第七輯. p.130. "帝出乎震 齊乎巽, 相見乎離, 到役乎坤, 說評兌, 戰乎乾, 勞乎坎, 成言乎艮. 萬物生乎震, 震東方也, 齊乎巽, 巽東南也, 齊也者, 言萬物之潔齊也, 離也者明也, 萬物皆相見, 南方之卦也, 聖人, 南面而聽天下嚮明而治, 蓋取諸此也, 坤也者地也, 萬物皆致養焉, 故曰致役乎坤, 兌, 正秋也, 萬物之所說也, 故曰說言乎兌, 戰于乾乾, 西北之卦也, 言陰陽相薄也, 坎者, 水也, 正北方之卦也, 勞卦也, 萬物之所歸也 故曰勞乎坎, 艮, 東北之卦也, 萬物之所成終而 所成始也, 故曰成言乎艮".

31. Kim, Hyuck Jae, ibid. p. 363, p. 391.

32. Lee, Sang Eun,
李相殷, 聖學十圖譯解, 上同. p.15. 太極圖解의 原文에는 "太極動而生陽, 動極而靜, 靜而生陰, …… 一動一靜, 互爲其根, 分陰分陽, 陽儀立焉, 陽變陰合, 而生・水・火・木・金・土, 五氣順布, 四時行焉, …… 五行之生也, 各一其種. 無極之眞, 二五之精, 妙合而凝 乾道成男 坤道成女, 二氣交感, 萬物化生, 萬物生生, 而變化無窮焉"라고 되어있다. 李相殷의 解說에 의하면 "太極이 動하여 陽을 生하고 動이 極하면 靜하나니 靜하여 陰을 生한다. …… 한번 動하고 한번 靜함이 서로 뿌리가 되어 陰으로 갈리고 陽으로 갈리니 兩儀가 맞서게 된다. 陽이 變하고 陰이 合하여 水・火・木・金・土를 生하니, 五氣가 순차로 펴지어 四時가 돌아가게 된다. 五行의 生함이 각각 그 性을 하나씩 가지니 無極의 眞과 二・五의 精이 妙合하여 凝結된다. 乾道는 男이 되고 坤道는 女가 되어 두 氣가 서로 感하여 萬物이 化生한다. 萬物이 生하고 生하니 變化는 다함이 없다."

Tai Chi moves and creates the Yang. When it moves extremely it becomes static and static Tai Chi creates the Yin. When it becomes static extremely it starts to move again. The alternation of one movement period and one static period divides the Yin and the Yang, and they oppose and confront each other. Yang's variation and Yin's combination create the five elements—the water, the fire, the wood, the metal, the soil. These five elements circulate in regular order, so the four seasons circulate. The five elements are one of Yin-Yang, Yin-Yang is a Tai

Chi, and Tai Chi is Wu Chi, primarily. (The origin of Tai Chi is Wu Chi.) Each of the five elements has one particular characteristic. The sincerity of Wu Chi and the spirits of two and five (陰陽, 水, 火, 木, 金, 土) coagulate in a peculiar way. A lump of Kan element becomes male and a lump of Kun element becomes female, two lumps of spirits respond to each other and create all things. The continuous creations cause the continuous change.

33. Han, Dong Suek,
   韓東錫, 宇宙變化의 原理, 上同. pp.293~295. 여기서는 金一夫의 三極説을 主張한다.
34. Kang, Chuen Bong, 姜天奉, "啓蒙傳疑硏究" 退溪學報, 第5·6輯. p.185.
35. Sim, Jong Chuel, *Chou I*, ibid. p. 292.
36. Kim, Hyuck Jae, ibid. p. 404.
37. Kim, Hyuck Jae, ibid. p. 178.
38. Kim, Hyuck Jae, ibid. p. 299
   上同. p.299. "彖曰 歸妹는 天地之大義也이니 天地不交而萬物이 不興하나니 歸妹는 人之終始也이라", 沈鑽哲, 上同. p.311. p.242.
39. Kim, Hyuck Jae, ibid. p. 360, Sim, Jong Chuel, ibid. p. 292
   金赫濟, 上同. p.360, 沈鑽哲, 上同. p.292. "此窮理之事 以者聖人以易之書也. 易者陰陽而已 幽明死生鬼神皆 陰陽之變天地之道也. 天文則有晝夜上下地理則 有南北高深 原者推之於則反者 要之於後 陰精陽氣 聚而成物之伸也 魂遊 魄降散而爲變鬼之歸也" 여기서 말하는 鬼神이란 사람이 죽은 뒤에 骨肉은 땅으로 돌아가고 精神은 하늘로 돌아간다는 이른 중에 精魄은 陰氣에 獨處하여 의존할바 없음으로 鬼라 이르고, 靈明한 陽物은 神이라 하여 鬼神이라고 한다. 또한 易에서는 陰陽變化의 헤아릴 수 없는 것을 神이라고 한다. (陰陽不測之謂神) 退溪는 神을 세 가지로 分類하되 그 理致는 같다고 하니, 朱子의 動無動靜 無靜의 神, 晦庵의 五行의 神, 子思의 神之格思의 神, 孔子의 無方體의 神등은 理가 氣를 타고 出入하는 在天의 神이고, 程子의 凝神의 神, 張子의 心神의 神, 晦庵의 在人爲理의 神과 心神安定의 神등은 사람에 있어서의 神이며, 精神이나 魂魄에서 神과 魂은 陽, 精과 魄은 陰을 뜻하는 것으로서, 鬼는 陰, 神은 陽을 뜻하는 祭祀의 神을 뜻하니 이 陰陽의 結合을 鬼神이라고 하고, 또한 鬼神을 통칭하여 神이라고 풀이했다. 姜天奉, 退溪學報 第三輯, pp.120. 淸의 王夫之는 死는 無로 돌아가는 것이 아니니, 生이란 陰陽의 變化로 完成된 것이고 死란 원래의 陰陽狀態로 돌아갈 뿐 消滅은 아닌 것이며, 다른 형태로 변화될 뿐이라고 주장하였다. 沈鑽哲, 上同. p.292.

40. Han, Dong Suek, ibid. p. 88.
41. Kim, Hyuck Jae, ibid. p. 353.
   金赫濟, 周易, p.353. 天尊地卑 乾坤定矣 卑高以陳 貴賤位矣 動靜有常 剛柔斯矣 方以類聚 物以群 吉凶生矣 在天成象 在地成形 變化見矣. 是故 剛柔相摩 八卦相盪.
42. Kim, Hyuck Jae,
   金赫濟, 上同. p.399. 日往則月來 月往則日來 日月相推而 明生焉 寒往則暑來 暑往則寒來 寒暑相推 而歲成焉 往者屈也 來者信也 屈信相感而 利生焉.

43. Kim, Hyuck Jae, ibid. p. 399.
   (天下同歸而殊途一致而百慮天下何思何慮)
44. Kang, Chuen Bong. 姜天奉, "啓蒙傳疑研究" 退溪學報, 第四輯, p.122.
45. Kim, Hyuck Jae,
   金赫濟, 上同. p.127. 象曰頤中有物일세 曰 噬嗑이니 噬嗑하여 而亨하니라. 剛柔가 分하여 動而明하고 雷電이 合而章하고.
46. Kim, Hyuck Jae,
   金赫濟, 上同. p.210. 沈鐘哲, 上同. p.177. 象曰睽는 火動而上하고 澤動而下하며 二女가 同居하나 其志가 不同行하나라. 說而麗乎明하고 柔가 進而上行하야 得中而應乎剛이라 是以小事吉이니라. 天地가 睽而其事이 同也이며 男女가 睽而其志이 通也이며 萬物이 睽而其事가 類也이니 睽之時用이 大矣哉라. 沈鐘哲은 註解에서 다음과 같이 睽를 풀이하고 있다. "睽는 反目, 外面한다는 뜻. 上卦는 火, 下卦는 못물이니, 물과 불은 性質이 相反되어 合할 수 없다. ☲는 中女, ☱는 少女의 형상으로 두 여자가 同居하면 반드시 反目함으로 睽라 한다. 서로 外面하고 反目하는 상태에서 吉하다고 볼 수 없다. 然이나 離는 밝은 덕이 있고 兌는 喜悅하므로 外面에서는 一致하고 있음으로 적은 일은 吉하다고 表象하였다." "이 社會에는 서로 相反된 矛盾 속에서 어긋나지만 一致點이 있다. 하늘은 높고 땅은 낮으나 萬物을 生成하는 것은 같고, 男女가 體質上으로는 다르나 愛情은 通한다. 그리고 萬物은 제각기 相反된 形體를 가지고 있으나 陰陽의 氣를 받아 成長하는 것은 같다. 그래서 서로 矛盾된 속에서도 합치고 어그러지는 것을 뜻한것이다. 意圖는 같으나 處世方法은 다르고 追求하는 것은 같으나 學說은 다르다."

Sim Jong Chuel explained the Kuei. "Kuei (睽) means antagonism or turning away. The upper trigram is fire, the lower trigram is pond water. The natures of the fire and water are contrary to each other, so they can not unify. ☲, 火 is the middle daughter, ☱, 兌 is the young daughter. If two women live together, they are antagonistic, so it is Kuei. Because they are antagonistic and turn away from each other they will not bring good luck. But because the fire (火) has bright virtue and the pond (兌) is joyous, it will result in good luck in small affairs. Even though there are contradictions and antagonism in human society, there are some accord points. Even though the heaven is high and the earth is low, they are the same in the creation of things. Even though the male and female have different natures, they are the same in loving. Even though all the things in the universe have different natures and many of them are contrary to each other, all of them are growing through the action of the Yin-Yang elements. Therefore, they can unify under the antagonistic conditions and they can act contrary to each other within the same world. They take different means for the same end and they have different theories for the same goal."

47. Kim, Hyuck Jae,
   金赫濟, 上同. pp.393. 神農氏没커늘 皇帝堯舜氏作하야 通其變하야 使民不倦하며 神而化之하야 使民宜之하니 易이 窮則變하고 變則通하고 通則久이라.
48. Kim, Hyuck Jae,
   金赫濟, 上同. p.416. 沈鐘哲, 上同. p.330. 變動은 以利言하고 吉凶은 以情遷이라 是故로 愛惡이 相攻而吉凶이 生하며 遠近이 相取而悔吝이 生하며 情僞가 相感而利害이 生하나니. 凡易之情이 近而不相得하면 則凶或害之하며 悔且吝하나니라.

49. Kim, Hyuck Jae,
    金赫濟, 上同. p.30. 天地變化하면 草木이 蕃하고 天地閉하면 賢人이 隱하나니. 沈鐘哲, 上同. p.42, p.278.
50. Sim, Jong Chuel, ibid. p. 100.
51. See the figure of the alternate creation of Yin-Yang.
52. Kim, Hyuck Jae, 金赫濟, 周易, 繫辭上傳. 第九章 p.371,
    Kang, Chuen Bong, 姜天奉 退溪學報 第三輯, p.76.
53. Kang, Chuen Bong, 姜天奉, 退溪學報 第三輯, p.120.
54. Kim, Hyuck Jae, ibid.
    周易의 繫辭上傳 第9章~第12章에서는 數의 變化, 八卦生成등 變化自體를 神秘的 것으로 表現하고 鬼神의 일로 귀착시켜서 聖人이라야 그 變化를 헤아릴 수 있음을 여러곳에서 표현하고 있다. 또한 占에서 사용하는 蓍와 河圖의 根源인 龍馬, 洛書의 根源인 龜甲을 神物로 다루고 있다.
55. Kang Chuen Bong, 姜天奉, 退溪學報 第三輯, p.120~125.
56. Kang Chuen Bong,
    姜天奉, "啓蒙傳疑硏究" 退溪學報 第九輯, pp.93~96. 여기서 奇偶란 첫번째 用事에서 5나 9가 나오고, 두번째와 세번째는 4나 8이 나오는데, 첫번째 用事에서 1을 빼면 모두가 4나 8이 된다. 그것을 4로 나누면 1이나 2가 나오는데 1이면 奇가 되고 2이면 偶가 된다. 즉 9·8·8이면 三偶로써 老陰이 되고, 5·4·4면 三奇로써 老陽이 되며, 9·8·4나 9·4·8이나 5·8·8이면 二偶一奇로 少陽이 되고, 9·4·4나 5·8·4나 5·4·8이면 二奇一偶로 少陰이 된다는 뜻이다.
57. Kang, Chuen Bong,
    姜天奉, "啓蒙傳疑硏究" 退溪學報 第七輯, p.127. "兄此四位, 陽中有陰, 陰中有陽, 四位子午卯酉, 四正位也, 午陽位之極, 而一陰生, 子陰位之極, 而一陽生, 二位陽中有陰, 陰中有陽固也, 卯位正東, 陽方中而未極, 西位正西, 陰方中而未極, 陽未極則陰在其中可知, 陰未極則陽在其中可知, 蒼蒼天地間無截然爲 陽爲陰之理, 故或以一極一生, 取在其中之義, 或以一未極, 取一在其中之義, 皆無所不可也."
58. Sim, Jong Chuel, ibid. p. 73. Kim, Hyuck Jae, ibid. p. 81.
    沈鐘哲, 上同. p.73. 金赫濟, 上同. p.81. "无平不陂며 无往不復이니 艱貞이면 无咎하야 勿恤이라도 其孚이라"
59. Sim, Jong Chuel, ibid. p. 100. Kim, Hyuck Jae. Ibid. p. 114
    "疊壤之極亂當復治"
60. Lee, Sang Eun, 李相殷, 聖學十圖譯解, 上同. p.15.
61. Lee, Sang Eun, ibid. p. 15-16.
62. Kim, Hyuck Jae, ibid. p. 365.
    金赫濟, 上同, p.365, "變通은 配四時하고 陰陽之義는 配日月하고"
63. Kim, Hyuck Jae, ibid. p. 398.
    金赫濟, 上同, p.398, "日往則月來하고 月往則日來하야 日月相推而 明生焉하며 寒往則暑來하고 暑往則寒來하야 寒暑가 相推而歲成焉하니 往者는 屈也이오 來者는 信也이니 屈信이 相感而利生焉하나니라."

64. Kim, Hyuck Jae, ibid. p. 305. Hellmut Wilhelm, THE I CHING, Princeton University Press, New Jersey, 1967, p. 670.
   金赫濟, 上同, p.305, "日中則昃하며 月盈則食하나니 天地盈虛도 與時消息이요 而況於人乎이며 況於鬼神乎여"
65. Kim, Hyuck Jae, ibid. p. 7. 金赫濟, 上同, p.7. "盈不可久也"
66. Kim, Hyuck Jae, ibid. p. 142.
   金赫濟, 上同, p.142, "反復其道 七日來復은 天行也이오"
67. Han, Dong Suek, ibid. p. 299.
68. Han, Dong Suek, ibid. p. 306-334.
69. Sim, Jong Chuel, ibid. p. 72
   沈鐘哲, 上同, p.72, "象曰天地交가 泰이니" "天地가 交而萬物이 通也이며, 上下가 交而其志가 同也이라."
70. Sim, Jong Chuel, ibid. p. 78.
   沈鐘哲, 上同, p.78, "象曰天地不交가 否이니" "則是天地가 不交而 萬物이 不通也이며 上下가 不交而天下가 无邦也이라"
71. Sim, Jong Chuel, ibid. p. 89.
   沈鐘哲, 上同, p.89, "象曰謙亨은 天道가 下濟而光明하고 地道가 卑而上行이라. 天道는 虧盈而益謙하고 地道는 變盈而流謙하고 鬼神은 害盈而福謙하고 …, 謙은 尊而光하고, 卑而不可踰이니 君子之終也이라"
72. Sim, Jong Chuel, ibid. p. 55-56.
   沈鐘哲, 上同, p.55, 56, "象曰天與水違行이 訟이니" "訟有孚窒惕"
73. Sim, Jong Chuel, ibid. p 149-150.
   上同 pp.149~150, "象曰咸은 感也이니 柔上而剛下하야 二氣가 感應以相與하야. 止而說하고 男下女이라, 是以亨利貞取女吉也이니라. 天地가 感而萬物이 化生하고 聖人이 感人心而天下和平하나니, 觀其所感而天地萬物之情을 可見矣리라."
74. Sim, Jong Chuel, ibid. p. 177. Kang, Chuen Bong.
   沈鐘哲, 上同, p.177, 姜天奉, 退溪學報 第九輯 pp.104~105, "象曰 上火下澤이 睽이니. 象曰 睽는 火動而上하고 澤動而下하며 二女同居하나 其志不同行하니라.
75. Sim, Jong chuel, ibid. p. 82.
   沈鐘哲, 上同, p.82, "天與火同人이니 君子以하야 類族으로 辨物하나리라"
76. Sim, Jong Chuel, ibid. p. 96.
   沈鐘哲, 上同, p.96, "剛來而下柔하고 動而說이 隨이니"
77. Sim Jong Chuel, ibid. p. 205.
   沈鐘哲, 上同, p.205, "萃聚也이니 順而說하고 剛中而應이라 故로 聚也이니라"
78. Sim, Jong Chuel, ibid. p. 43. Kang, Chuen Bong.
   沈鐘哲, 上同, p.43, 姜天奉, 退溪學報 第九輯 p.98, "屯은 剛柔가 始交而難生하며 動乎險中하니 大亨貞이니라"
79. Sim, Jong Chuel, ibid. p. 111.
   沈鐘哲, 上同, p.111, "頤中有物일세 曰 噬嗑이니 噬嗑하야 而亨하나리라. 剛柔分하고 動而明하고 雷電이 合而章하고 柔得中而上行하니 雖不當位나 利用獄也이니라.

80. Sim, Jong Chuel, ibid. p. 91.
   沈鐘哲, 上同. p.91. "六五는 不當以其隣이니 利用侵伐이니 无不利하리라. 象曰利用侵伐은 征不服也이라."
81. Sim, Jong Chuel, ibid. p. 148.
   沈鐘哲, 上同. p.148. "上九는 王用出征이며 有嘉이니 折首코 獲匪其醜이면 无咎이리라. 象曰王用出征은 以正邦也이라"
82. Sim, Jong Chuel, ibid. p. 198.
83. Sim, Jong Chuel, ibid. p. 222.
   沈鐘哲, 上同. p.222. "革은 水火가 相息하며 二女가 同居하되 其志不相得이 曰革이라. 己日乃孚는 革而信之라 文明以說하야 大亨以正하니, 革而當할세 其悔가 乃亡하니라. 天地가 革而四時成하며 湯武가 革命하여 順乎天而應乎人하니 革之時가 大矣哉라."
84. Kim, Hyuck Jae,
   金赫濟, 原本備旨 大學中庸, 明文堂, 서울: 1986. 大學章句 pp.9~12. "大學之道는 在明明德하며 在親民하며 在止於至善이니라" 註解, 大學者, 大人之學也, 明明之也, 明德者, 人之所得乎天, 而虛靈不昧, 而具衆理, 而應萬事者也, 但, 爲氣稟所拘, 人欲所蔽, 則有時而昏, 然, 基本體之明則有未嘗息者, 故學者, 當因其所發而遂明之, 以復其初也. 新者, 革其舊之謂也, 言, 既自明其明德, 又當推以及人, 使之亦有以去, 其舊染之汚也, 止者, 必至於是, 而不遷之意, 至善則事理, 當然之極也, 言, 明明德新民, 皆當止於至善之地, 而不遷蓋必其有以盡夫, 天理之極, 而無一毫人欲之私也. 三者大學之綱領也. 金赫濟, 上同, 中庸章句, pp.2~5, "天命之謂性이요 率性之謂道이요 修道之謂教이니라." 命, 猶令也, 性, 即理也, 天以陰陽五行, 化生萬物, 氣以成形而理亦賦焉, 猶命令也, 於是, 人物之生, 因各得其所賦之理, 以爲健順五常之德, 所謂性也. 金赫濟, 原本集註 周易, 上同, p.8., "君者行此四德者라 故로 曰乾元亨利貞이라" "夫大人者는 與天地合其德하며" 元者生物之始 天地之德 莫先於此 故於 時爲春於 人則爲仁而衆善之長也, 亨者生物之通物至於此莫 不嘉美故於時爲夏於 人則爲禮而衆美之會也, 利者生物之遂物各得宜不相妨害 故於時爲秋於人則爲 義而順其分之和, 貞者生物之成實理具備 隨在各足, 故於 時爲冬 於人 則爲智而爲衆事之 幹幹木之身而 枝葉所依以立者也.
85. Kim, Hyuck Jae, ibid. Many hexagrams praised the middle line. The second line of the Hsu hexagram (需卦) is good luck in the medium, even though there are some fault findings, and the fifth line will be lucky if he waits at the medium. The Sung hexagram (訟卦) is dangerous, but the fifth line will be good luck if he judges impartially at the medium. The second line of the Shih hexagram (師卦) is lucky because he stays mid-way. The fifth line of the Pi hexagram (比卦) is good luck because sturdiness is in the medium. The Hsiao Chu hexagram (小畜卦) is also good luck because sturdiness is in the medium. The fifth line of the Lü hexagram (履卦) will not be shameful even if he takes the king's position because he is in the medium. The second line of the Tai hexagram (泰卦) will be beneficial if he carries out the middle line, the fourth line is trustful without precaution because his mind is in the moderate condition, and the fifth line will take great luck because he performs his will of medium. The Pi hexagram (否卦) is an ill-luck hexagram, but only the fifth

line is lucky at the medium. The Tung Jên hexagram (同人卦) goes thoroughly because they accomplish the great union at the medium. The Ta Yu (大有卦) hexagram does not collapse because it loads in the middle and the second line sustains for a long time in the middle. The second line of the Ku hexagram (蠱卦) straightens the mother's fault with the middle line. The people will trustingly respect the king because the fifth line of the Kuan hexagram (觀卦) maintains the medium and justice (中正). The fifth line of the Fu hexagram (復卦) carries out self-accomplishment by the middle line. The second line of the Ta Chü (大畜卦) hexagram stops by himself because he is in the middle. The second and the fifth lines of the Ta Kuo hexagram (大過卦) go forward easily because the Yang lines are in the middle. The Li hexagram (離卦) goes through because mildness is in the middle. The second line of the Hsien hexagram (咸卦) will be safe as long as he holds his position. The fifth line of the Tun hexagram (遯卦) escapes easily because he reacts as a middle line. Even though the second line of the Ta Chung hexagram (大壯卦) is in an inconvenient situation, he will be ultimately benefit through the virtue of medium. The second line of the Chin hexagram (晉卦) receives great fortune because he is in the middle. The Kuei hexagram (睽卦) does not express regret because the fifth line reacts to the second line in the middle position. The fifth line of the Chien hexagram (蹇卦) is beautiful because he is at the medium and the justice (中正). All lines gather together in the Tsui hexagram (萃卦) because the sturdiness is in the middle. Everything goes through at the Shêng hexagram (升卦) because the sturdiness reacts as middle. The only great man is good luck in the Kun hexagram (困卦) because the sturdiness is in the middle. The fifth line of the Chên hexagram (震卦) will not lose much because he is in the middle. The fifth line of the Chieh hexagram (節卦) can go through because it is in the medium. Because the second line of the Chi Chi hexagram (既濟卦) is in the middle, it is initially good luck. Because the fifth line of the Wei Chi hexagram (未濟卦) is in the middle, it goes through. It is the explanation of *Chou I* that great accomplishment is possible in the middle condition, no matter what the character the hexagram may be, or whether the line is Yin or Yang. Even in the difficult situations one can avoid big disaster if he is in the middle. That is the *Chou I*'s analysis.

86. Kim, Hyuck Jae, 金赫濟, 原本備旨 中庸, p.14; p.15, p.17· p.22. 第四章, "子曰 道之不行也를 我知之矣로라, 知者는 過之하고 愚者는 不及也이니라, 道之不明也를 我知之矣로라, 賢者는 過之하고 不肖者는 不及也이니라." 同, 第六章, "子曰 舜은 其大知也與이신져, 舜이 好問而好察, 邇言하시되, 隱惡而揚善하시며, 執其兩端하셔 用其中於民하시니 其斯以爲舜乎이신져, 同解說, 舜之所以爲大知者, 以其不自用 而取諸人也, 邇言者, 淺近之言, 猶必察焉, 其無遺善, 可知, 言之未善者則, 隱度不宣, 其善者則播而不匿, 其廣大光明, 又如此則人孰不樂告以善哉, 兩端, 謂衆論不同之極致, 蓋凡物, 皆有兩端, 如小大厚薄之類, 於善之中, 又執其兩端而量度, 以取中然後, 用之則其擇之審而行之至矣, 然, 非在我之權度, 精切不差, 何以與此, 此, 知之所以 無過不及而道之所以行也.

87. Kim, Hyuck Jae,
    金赫濟, 上同, p.9. pp.14. 喜怒愛樂, 情也, 其未發則性也, 無所偏倚故, 謂之中, 發皆中節, 情之正也 無所乖戾 故, 謂之和, 大本者, 天命之性, 天下之理, 皆由比出, 道之體也, 達道者, 循性之謂, 天下古令之所共由, 道之用也, 此言性情之德, 以明道不可離之意.

88. Lee, Sang Eun,
    李相殷, 退溪의 生涯와 學問, 서울 : 退溪學研究院
    李相殷, 聖學十圖譯解, 서울 : 退溪學研究院

89. Kim, Hyuck Jae, Sim, Jong Chuel,
    金赫濟, 原本輯註 周易, 서울 : 明文堂, 1987, p.8, 沈鐘哲, 周易, 上同, p.26. "元者는 善之長也이오, 亨者는 嘉之會也이요, 利者는 義之和也이오, 貞者는 事之幹也이니, 君子는 體仁이 足以長人이며, 嘉會가 足以合體이며 利物이 足以和義이며 貞固가 足以幹事이니"라고 表現하고, 그 解義에서 貞者生物之成實 現具備隨在各足 故於時爲冬於 側爲智而 爲衆事之 幹幹木之身而枝葉 所依以立春也라고 貞을 풀이함.

90. Kim, Hyuck Jae, ibid. p. 356.
    金赫濟, 上同, p.356. 聖人이 設卦하야 觀象繫辭焉하야 而明吉凶하며 剛柔相推하야 而生變化하니 是故로 吉凶者는 失得之象也이요, 同, p.385, 吉凶者는 言乎其失得也이요, 同, p.390, 吉凶者는 貞勝者也. 同, p.41, 直은 其正也오 方은 其義也니. 同, p.59, 貞은 正也니.

91. Kim, Hyuck Jae,
    中庸 第二十章 "故 爲政이 在人하니 取人以身이오 修身以道요 修道以仁이니라"

92. Kim, Hyuck Jae,
    論語, 爲政篇, "子曰 爲政以德이면 譬如北辰이 居其所어든 而衆星共之니라. 道之以政 齊之以刑 民免而無恥니라 道之以德하고 齊之以禮면 有恥且格이니라".

93. Kim, Hyuck Jae,
    孟子, 公孫丑章句上, 第三節, "孟子曰 以力假仁者는 霸니 霸必有大國이오 以德行仁者는 王이니 王不待大라 湯이 以七十里하시고 文王이 以百里하시니라. 以力服人者는 非心服也라 力不贍也오 以德服人者는 中心이 悅而誠服也니 如七十子之服孔子也라 詩云 自西 自東하며 自南自北이 無思不服이라하니 此之謂也니라.

94. Lee, Sang Eun,
    李相殷, 聖學十圖譯解, 退溪學研究院, p.54, 55. "朱子曰, 仁者, 天地生物之心 而人之所得以爲心. 未發之前, 四德具焉, 而惟仁則包乎四者……己發之際, 四端著焉, 而惟惻隱 則貫乎四端, …

95. Kang, Chuen Bong, 姜天奉, 上同, 退溪學報 第3輯, p.124.

96. Sim, Jong Chuel, ibid. p. 9.

97. Kim, Hyuck Jae, ibid. p. 21, p. 27.
    金赫濟, 上同, p.21., p.27. "先하면 迷하고 後하면 得하리니 主利하니라." "上六은 龍戰于野하니 其血玄黃이로다. 象曰 龍戰于野는 其道가 窮也이라"

98. Sim, Jong Chuel, ibid. p. 41-42.
    沈鍾哲, 上同, pp.41~42. "隱雖有迷나 含之하야 以從王事하야 弗敢成也이니" "陰疑於陽하면 必戰하나니 爲記力嫌於无陽也어라"
99. Kang, Chuen Bong,
    姜天奉, 退溪學報 第十二輯, 上同, p.81
100. Kang, Chuen Bong,
    姜天奉, 退溪學報 第十輯. p.102.
101. Sim, Jong Chuel, ibid. p. 103, p. 158.
102. Kang, Chuen Bong,
    姜天奉, 退溪學報 第九輯, pp.103, 104.
103. Kim, Hyuck Jae, ibid. p. 78-84, Sim, Jong Chuel, ibid. p. 73-78
    金赫濟, 上同, pp.78~84, 沈鍾哲, 上同, pp.73~78, "泰는 小往코 大來하니 吉하야 亨하나라. 象曰 泰小往大來吉亨은 則是 天地가 交而萬物이 通也이며 上下가 交而其志이 同也이라. 內陽而外陰하야 內健而外順하며 內君子而外小人하니 君子의 道는 長하고 小人의 道는 消也이라". "否之匪人이니 不利君子貞하니 大往小來니라. 象曰 否之匪人 不利君子貞, 大往小來는 則是天地가 不交而萬物이 不通也이며, 上下가 不交 而天下가 无邦也이라. 內陰而外陽하며 內柔而外剛하며 內小人而外君子하니, 小人道는 長하고 君子道는 消也니라.
104. Kang, Chuen Bong, 姜天奉, 退溪學報 第九輯, pp.99~100.
105. Sim, Jong Chuel, ibid. p. 118.
106. Sim, Jong Chuel, ibid. p. 137.
    沈鍾哲, 上同, p.137, "大過는 棟이 橈이니, … 象曰 大過는 大者가 過也이오 棟橈는 本末이 弱也이라" "九三은 棟이 橈이니 凶하니라. 象曰棟橈之凶은 不可以有輔也일새라, 上六은 過涉滅頂이라 凶하니 无咎하니라."
107. Kang, Chuen Bong, 姜天奉, 退溪學報 第九輯, p.102. p.130.
108. Kim, Hyuck Jae,
    金赫濟, 上同, pp.337, "小過는 亨하니 利貞하니 可小事이오 不可大事이니 飛鳥遺之音에 不宜上이오 宜下이면 大吉하리라."
109. Kang, Chuen Bong, ibid.
110. Sim, Jong Chuel, ibid. p. 197.
    沈鍾哲, 上同, p.197, "夬는 揚于王庭이니 孚號有厲이니라 告自邑이오 不利卽戎이며 利有攸往하니라".
111. Kang, Chuen Bong, 姜天奉, 退溪學報 第九輯, pp.105~106.
112. Kim, Hyuck Jae, ibid. p. 182.
    金赫濟, 上同, p.182, "象曰恒은 久也이니, 剛上而柔下하고 雷風이 相與하고 巽而動하고 剛柔가 皆應이 恒이니 恒亨无咎利貞은 久於其道也이니 天地之道가 恒久而不已也이니라. 利有攸往은 終則有始이 일세니라, 日月이 得天而能久照하며 四時가 變化而能久成하며 聖人이 久於其道而天下가 化成하나니, 觀其所恒而天地萬物之情을 可見矣리라. 象曰雷風이 恒이니 君子가 以하여 立不易方하나니라." "恒常久也 爲卦震剛在上巽柔在下震巽巽二物相與巽 順震動 爲巽而動 二體六爻陰陽相應 四者理之常 故爲恒其占爲 能久於其道 則亨而无咎 然又必利於守貞則乃爲得 所常久之道 利利有攸往也".

113. Kim, Hyuck Jae, ibid p. 206.
 金赫濟, 上同. p.206. "象曰 家人은 女가 正位乎內하고 男이 正位乎外하니 男女正이 天地之大義也이라. 家人이 有嚴君焉하니 父母之謂也이라. 父父子子兄兄弟弟夫夫婦婦而家道가 正하리니 正家而天下가 定矣리라".

114. Sim, Jong Chuel, ibid.
 沈鍾哲, 上同, p.34, 夫大人者는 與不地合其德하며 與日月合其明하여 與四時合其序하며 與鬼神合其吉凶하며 先天而天不違하여 後天而奉天時하나니 天且弗違은 而況於人乎이며 況於鬼神乎이여.

115. Sim, Jong Chuel, ibid. p. 8.
116. Kim, Hyuck Jae, ibid. p. 360.
 金赫濟, 上同. p.360. "易이 與天地準이라 故로 能彌綸天地之道하나니 仰以觀於天文하고 俯以察於地理라 是故로 知幽明之故하며 原始反終이라 故로 知死生之說하며 精氣爲物이오 游魂爲變이라. 是故로 知鬼神之情狀하나니라. 與天地相似이라 故로 不違하나니 知周乎 萬物而道濟天下이라 故로 不過하며 旁行而不流하여 樂天知命이라 故로 不憂하며 安土하여 敦乎仁이라 故로 能愛하나니라. 範圍天地之化而不過하여 曲成萬物이 不遺하며 通乎晝夜之道而知라.

117. Kim, Hyuck Jae, ibid. p. 365.
 金赫濟, 上同. p.365. "廣大는 配天地하고 變通은 配四時하고 陰陽之義는 配日月하고 易簡之善은 配至德하나니라.

118. Kim, Hyuck Jae, ibid. p. 104.
 金赫濟, 上同, p.104, "象曰 豫는 剛應而志行하고 順以動이 豫라, 豫는 順以動이라 故로 日月이 不過四時가 不忒하고 聖人이 以順動이라 則刑罰이 淸而民이 服하나니 豫之時義가 大矣哉라.

119. If righteousness wins it is a good phenomenon. If one behaves according to the laws of nature, he can gain something. Gaining is good and losing is bad.

120. Sim, Jong Chuel, ibid. p. 34, Sim Jong Chuel said, "Heaven is indifferent, it changes thoughtlessly." The explanation of the Kan hexagram also said, "Human accords to the order of the heaven and the earth originally, but because the greediness shades the original mind in general, only the selfless saint can go through. Therefore, Ta Jên (大人) behaves according to the laws of nature."

121. Han Dong Suek, ibid. p. 306, p. 326. Ahn, Kyung Juen,
 安耕田, 개벽, 大原出版社, 1988, p.264.

Chapter 4

Political Change in the View of the Theory of Change (Chou I)

The Concept of Ta Hsiao (大小)

The words *Ta Hsiao* (大小), *Ta Jên* (大人), *Hsiao Jên*, (小人), and *Ta Tao* (大道) are used very often in *Chou I*, and the concept of Ta Hsiao described as a paired word is compared to the Yin-Yang concept. In chapter 3 of *Upper Chi* Tzu Chuan said, "There are big and small in a row in the Kua (齊小大者…卦有小大)" the Tai hexagram (泰卦) said, "small go, big come (小往大來)," the Pi hexagram (否卦), "big go, small come (大往小來)," the Ta Kuo hexagram (大過卦), "The big is excessive in Ta Kuo hexagram (大過大者過也)," and the Hsiao Kuo hexagram (小過卦), "The small is excessive, so it goes well, it is fortunate in small affairs, but the sturdiness lost it's po-sition and missed the medium, so it is impossible to do big affairs (小過小者過而亨也是以小事吉也剛失位而不中是以不可大事也)".[1]

The Tai hexagram (泰卦) shows that the upper three Yin lines retreat and the lower three Yang lines grow, while the Pi hexagram (否卦) shows that the upper three Yang lines retreat and the lower three Yin lines grow. The Ta Kuo hexagram (大過卦) shows the four Yang lines take the middle position and the Hsiao Kuo hexagram (小過卦) that the four Yin lines overpower the two Yang lines. When we observe these four hexagrams and generalize their explanations, it is very clear that the meaning of Ta and Hsiao is Yang and Yin. Ta is just Yang and Hsiao is just Yin.

The natures of Yin and Yang are explained as opposing each other. According to Shuo Kua Chuan (說卦傳), Kan is strong and Kun is mild (chapter 7), Kan is the head and Kun is the belly (chapter 9). Kan is heaven, therefore it is called the father; Kun is earth, therefore it is called the mother (chapter 10). Kan is heaven—it is a round thing, it is a king, the father, the jade, the metal, the coldness, the ice, the strong red, a good horse, an old horse, a lean horse, a wild horse, and the tree fruit. Kun is the earth—the mother, a cloth, a kettle, a miserliness, the evenness, a cow with calf, a large wagon, a design, a mass, a sack, a soil, and is black in color.[2] Sho Kua compared the natures of Yin and Yang as in the above description.

When we generalize the above explanation, Yang is manly, strong and sturdy, active, and goes forward. Yin is feminine, mild, passive, goes backward, and is steady. Therefore, Yang is the king and Yin is the subject. Yang is straight, impartial, and thoughtless; Yin is quiet, selfish, and moves powerfully. Yang opens and Yin shuts, Yang leads the creation and Yin completes the creation. The social meaning of the Ta Hsiao concept is similar to the concepts of public and private. Ta is public and Hsiao means private. This is the explanation of the fifth line of the Kan hexagram: "In general, the great man (大人) accords the virtue with the heaven and earth, accords the lightness with the sun and the moon, accords the good or ill luck with the four seasons. When he does in advance of the heaven, the heaven does not against him; when he goes behind the heaven, he accommodates to heaven. Even heaven does not do against him—how much less do man and Kuei Shen (鬼神)!"[3] In this context, "the great man" means a man who acts according to heaven's principles and who follows heaven's way.

The *Book of Great Learning* (大學章句) defined the Ta Hsüch (大學) as a science of Ta Jên (大人). The *Book of Great Learning* begins with teaching this: "The virtue of the great learning is on brightening the light virtue, renewing people with light virtue, and maintaining the state of extreme virtue (大學之道 在明明德 在親民 在止於至善). The brightening of light virtue means lightening the heaven-given virtues—the humanity, (仁) the righteousness (義), the courtesy (禮), the wisdom (智), and making an impartial man who has no private desires at all. The great learning is the science which emphasizes purely the public interest."[4]

On the other hand, the Chien hexagram (謙卦) emphasized the

impartial principle as the explanation of the king's way. Tuan Tzu and Hsiang Chuan of the Chien hexagram described, "modesty goes fairly well. The virtue of heaven goes downward and lightens brightly, and the virtue of the earth goes upward. Heaven hates the fullness and likes the modesty. The modesty is high and bright. Even though the modesty is low, one can not cross over, so it is a final goal of the king. According to Hsiang, the mountain is at the middle of the earth in the Chien hexagram, the king deducts from the fullness and adds to the lack, and also measures the balance and equalizes it."[5] The Chien hexagram defined the king's way as Ta Tao (大道).

The *Record of Courtesy* (禮記) also fully explained Ta Tao. The great equality chapter (大同章) of the *Record of Courtesy* said, "The deed of Ta Tao accepts the whole world as one public unit, selects the clever man and teaches the faith (trusty and justice) and trains the harmony. Therefore, people do not love only their own parents or children, an old person should have a place to complete his life, an adult person should have a place to work, children should have a place to grow, the widow, widower, solitudes, and sick persons should have a place to cultivate, man should have a position and woman should have a man to marry. It is bad thing to throw away property, but is not necessary to store it in his personal warehouse. The powerless are hateful, but the strength is not used only for himself. Therefore, the plot does not arise and there is no robber or rebellion, so one does not need to lock one's door. This state of society is called the society of the great equality (大同社會)."[6]

When we generalize the explanation of the Chi Tzu Chuan, the *Great Learning*, the Tuan and Hsiang of the Chien hexagram, and the great equality chapter of the *Record of Courtesy*, it is very clear that the social meaning of Ta Tao is the public drive. The action that deduces the fullness and adds to the lack, and equalizes distribution of things, are the public interests of impartiality and co-existence. The man who is extremely impartial and who has no private desire at all is a great man (大人) who is full of public spirit and performs only in the public interest.

Defining the whole world as one public unit introduces a kind of universalism that crosses over race and national boundaries. The thought that widows, widowers, solitudes, and sick persons should have a place to cultivate is a kind of pan-humanism and of socialism. The spirit where one's strength is not used only for oneself implies social service and sacrifice, so it is a spirit of humanity and public interest. In addition, the Ta Tao is defined as heaven's way. In other words, heaven's doctrine (virtue) is rearing all the people evenly and the man who follows heaven's doctrine is a Ta Jên (大人) or a king (君子).

If Ta (大) is public and Hsiao (小) is private, Ta Tao (大道) is the public way and Hsiao Tao (小道) is the private way. Ta Jên (大人) is a public worker and Hsiao Jên (小人) is a private worker. So the Ta Tao is a kind of socialism and Hsiao Tao is similar to individualism.

Chou I insists upon the priority of public interest but it does not ignore the private interest, and expresses the importance of the private way. Tuan Tzu of the Kun hexagram (坤卦彖辭) said:

"Oh Kun Yüan (坤元) is extreme! All beings originate from this, Kun obeys the virtue of heaven. It has a liberal favour so it carries all things, its virtue harmonizes boundlessly and illuminates greatly, therefore everything goes through successfully."

"A mare is a kind of earth, roaming around the earth endlessly. If she is mild and does the right thing, she will be beneficial because she follows the king's way (君子之道). If she leads, the confusion will make her lose her way, but if she follows, she will receive the normal fairness. She gains friends in the southwest direction because she goes with her same kind; losing friends in the northeast direction means great fortune after all. If she is steady and straight, she will have good luck. The reason for her good fortune is because she accommodates to the virtue of earth."
7

The Kun way is a private way and the individual is the most basic origin of the birth, so there is nothing alive without the individual. Therefore, Kun is as important as Kan in creation, but when Kun goes with Kan, Kun does its share by accommodating Kan. The private way is docile but its action is strong; it is small but infiltrates without any empty openings, and it accomplishes things by itself.

As in the above explanation, *Chou I* defined the Yang as Ta (大) and the Yin as Hsiao (小), Ta as public and Hsiao as private, and it described their relationships as being compatible. Therefore, the Ta (大) means public, public interest, and socialism, while the Hsiao (小) means private, private interest, and individualism.

Ta Hsiao Reaction and Political Change

When Ta means public and Hsiao means private—when Ta Tao means socialism and Hsiao Tao means individualism—the concept of Ta Hsiao becomes a political concept and the change according to the Ta Hsiao reaction becomes political change. Hsing Li Hsüch (性理學) treated the psychology of ancient Oriental society and Hsing Li Hsüch treated the public mind and private mind. Toegae also attempted to connect the human mind to the theory of Tai Chi, or the theory of Yin-Yang Wu Hang (陰陽五行說). According to him, each of the five elements (水, 火, 木, 金, 土) gives the human body one nature at birth—the humanity (仁) from the wood (木), the courtesy (禮) from the fire (火), the righteousness (義) from the metal (金), the wisdom (智) from the water (水), and the sincerity (信) from the soil (土). These minds are defined as a heaven-given mind (天性) or an original nature (本性). These original natures are metaphysical beings, so they cannot be identified. But when they are expressed as feelings, they appear as compassion (惻隱之心), refraining (辭讓之心), shamefulness (羞惡之心), propriety (是非之心), and sincerity (誠實之心). On the other hand, there are passions which arise from the human body when it is stimulated. Those passions are gladness (喜), anger (怒), grief (哀), fear (懼), love (愛), enmity (惡), and greed (慾).

The heaven-given natures that Toegae classified as original natures are similar to the public mind and the natures classified as passions are similar to the private mind. The original natures are called *heaven's mind* (天心), or Tao Hsin (道心), because these minds were given from heaven's virtue, and the passions are called *human's mind* (人心) because they arise from the human body. Concerning the relationship between original nature (道心) and passion (人心), Toegae understood that the original natures are fighting with the passions in the human mind. So man should train his mind so that the original mind controls the human passions. When the public minds control the private mind completely, one becomes a saint.

Toegae's theory is similar to the developed theory of moderation. The *Book of Moderation* explained, "The feelings (gladness, anger, grief, pleasure) are not expressed in the condition of the middle line, and even if these feelings are expressed, they stop at the middle in the condition of harmony (喜怒哀樂之未發謂之中 發而皆中節謂之和)." The goal of

Figure 4-1
The Figure of Mind that Penetrates the Original Nature and the Passion
心 統 性 情 圖

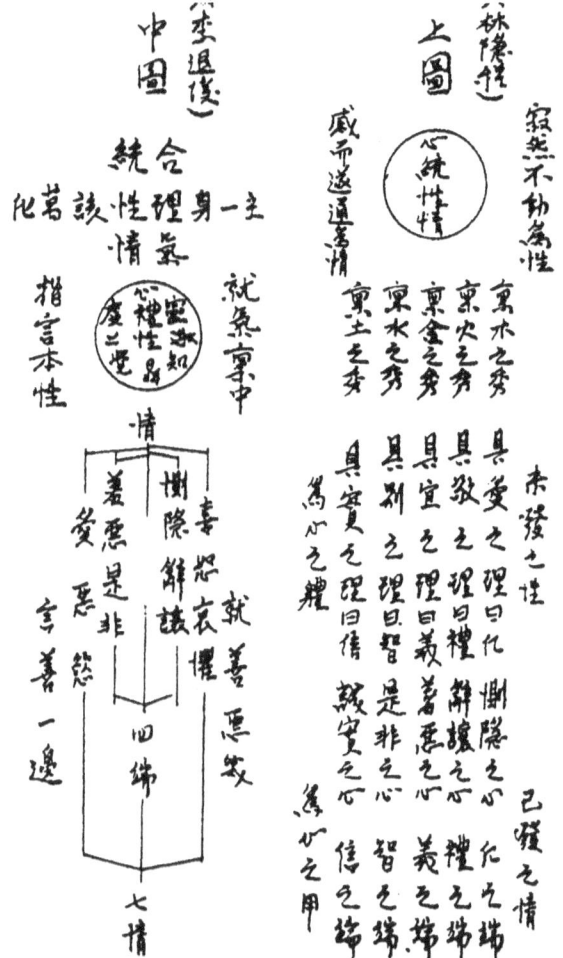

Material, Lee, Sang Eun, 李相殷, 聖學十圖譯解, 退溪學研究院, p.47

learning and training is to achieve the state of medium and harmony described in the *Book of Moderation*. Toegae's goal of mind training (敬) is an entry into that kind of harmony.

There are a few problems with Toegae's theory of the Union of Heaven's Mind and Human's Mind (天人心合一說). According to the theory of Yin-Yang Wu Hang, the wood element and the fire element are of Yang's nature and the metal element and the water element are of Yin's nature, the wood and fire elements are heaven's way and the metal and water elements are earth's way, and the wood and fire elements are public reason and the metal and water elements are private reason. But Toegae's theory does not follow this. According to Toegae, all four natures—humanity, righteousness, courtesy, and wisdom—stand for public reason. Because courtesy and wisdom came out of the Yin-natured water and metal elements, the theory does not seem reasonable.

According to the theory of Yin-Yang Wu Hang, human is one Tai Chi and the public and private minds co-exist in the human mind. Toegae, however, classified all the human mind (人心) as the private mind. Therefore, Toegae's theory of nature and passion needs to be studied more. Toegae's theory is difficult to use as an analytic tool of the relationship between public and private reason. When we apply the public-private concept to the theory of Tai Chi and Yin-Yang, the following hypotheses develop. First, the Yin and Yang elements are created alternately. If the Yang element grows and pushes out the Yin element, then the Yang element grows while the Yin element withers. When the Yang element is extreme the Yin element arises and grows and pushes out the Yang element. This process is repetitive and cyclical and is a natural phenomenon that cannot be stopped (nor can the direction be turned artificially). If we apply the concept of public and private to this phenomenon, it becomes: when the public strength grows and pushes out the private strength, the former grows and the latter withers. And when the public strength becomes extreme, the private strength arises and grows by pushing out the public. This process is also repetitive and cyclical and cannot be stopped nor have its direction turned artificially.

Second, the Yin-Yang elements do not exist apart—they stay together all the time. The Yang element contains the Yin element and vice-versa. Even though it looks like a Yang element from the outside, the Yin element is growing inside; even it though it looks like a Yin element from the outside, the Yang element is growing inside. When two Yang elements and one Yin element combine, the result is a Yin element, and when two Yin elements and one Yang element combine, a Yang element results. All things in nature are constructed by complicated combinations of the Yin and Yang elements, and appear with a Yin or a Yang nature. But a pure Yin element or a pure Yang element are extremely rare; most instances represent some combination of the two. When we explain this with respect to the concept of public and private, the private interest (私利) and the public interest (公利) exist, not apart from each other, but always together. The public interest contains private interest and the private interest contains public interest. When two public interests and one private interest combine, it becomes a private interest, and when two private interests and one public interest combine, it becomes a public interest. Even though it looks like a public interest from the outside looking in, the private interest is growing from inside and vice-versa. All the things in the nature are constructed by complicated combinations of private and public interests and appear as one or the other. Pure private interests or pure public interests are extremely rare; most are combinations.

These theories can be verified exactly in real life. When two personal interests combine, one public interest arises. All the persons in a family have their own personal interests, but when these personal interests combine, it becomes a family interest—a public interest of the entire family. But it acts as a private interest in the relationships with other families. For example, when the private interest of a husband and the private interest of a wife combine, it creates a public interest—a child. The creation of a child creates the private interest of a child, and creates the public interest of three persons. This is the start of the interest relationship. This interest relationship expands from family to village to society to state to world, and develops as a more complicated interest relationship. These interest groups express some private interests or public interests from the outside looking in, but they contain numerous private interests and public interests inside that are different from an outsider's point of view. Therefore, the public interest and the private interest do not exist apart—they exist together all the time.

Third, there is an expanding and diminishing phenomenon (盈虛消息現象) between the Yang element and the Yin element. When the Yang element prospers the Yin element declines; if the Yin element rises the Yang element falls. The period in which the Yang grows and the Yin dwindles is defined as a period of growth, while the period in which the Yin element expands and the Yang element declines is defined as a period of declination. When these theories are substituted with the concept of public and private, there are expanding and diminishing phenomenon between the public mind and the private mind. Therefore, when the public mind increases the private mind decreases; when the private mind increases the public mind decreases. This relationship is vicissitudinary so they effect each other in opposite ways. In political society the private interest and the public interest conflict with each other, so if the private interest expands, the public interest diminishes, and if the public interest grows, the private interest declines. When the public interest exceeds the private interest, a whole society can grow evenly. This time is defined as a period of growth. When the private interest exceeds the public interest, a few people can grow but the whole society fails to develop. Therefore, the vicissitude phenomenon of Yin-Yang can be applicable to political theory.

Fourth, the Yang element has a nature to move forward and the Yin element has a nature to go backward—the Yang starts creation and the Yin completes creation. So the public element has a nature to move forward and the private element has a nature to go backward—the public way starts creation and the private way completes creation. In reality, the increase in birth rates and population is carried out by the public interest, but a born person is living as a private person.

Fifth, the Yang element and the Yin element have the same origins but have different natures. The Yang element and the Yin element are heterogeneous and oppose each other even though their origins are the same, Tai Chi. So humans, as Tai Chi, have both the Yang and the Yin elements. When this principle is substituted with the concept of the private and the public, the public mind and the private mind are heterogeneous and oppose each other, but their origins are the same. A human who is considered as a small universe has both a public and a private mind; there is no person who has only a public mind or only a private mind. The public mind and the private mind are heterogeneous, but both arise from the same person. Therefore, man has both public and private minds and political society has both public and private interests.

Sixth, the Yin element and the Yang element have conflicting and contradictory natures. Change occurs when the Yin and the Yang elements line up. If there is no Yin-Yang there will be no change, and if Yin-Yang collapses there will be no change. Even though Yin and Yang conflict with each other, it is a co-pushing phenomenon in the process of the alternate creation; it is the process of preparation for future creation. Therefore, their relationship is a mutually aiding relationship, reciprocally infiltrating and endlessly circulating; it is not just a mutually negating struggle.

When we apply the public and private concept to this relationship, the public interest and the private interest have conflicting and contradictory natures. When public interest and private interests line up, change occurs. If there are no private or public interests, there will be no change, and if either collapse there will be no change. Even though the private interest and the public interest conflict with each other, it is a co-pushing phenomenon in the process of the alternate creation of the private interest and the public interest, and it is the process of preparation for future creation. Therefore, their relationship is a mutually aiding one, reciprocally infiltrating and endlessly circulating; it is not just a mutually negating struggle.

Toegae's theory that the private mind and public mind are fighting each other in the human mind is a theory of the psychological training of man. But because the conflict between the public mind and the private mind in society is a conflict between socialism and individualism, it is a core of politics. When politics is defined as an authoritative allocation of social values, politics cannot be considered without also considering the private and public interests, which can conflict with each other. Because the process of distribution is one of making agreements between the public interest and the private interest, conflict between the two is inevitable. Therefore, the conflict between individualism and socialism in the political field is not a mutually negating struggle, but is a mutually supporting relationship.

Creation

Just as the goal of the Yin-Yang movement is creation (in the theory of change), the goal of the interaction between the public and private interest is the creation of a human being. To say it another way, as the virtue of nature is the creation of all beings, the goal of politics is to rear human beings. The political problems are distribution problems and the distribution problems are public subjects. So the goal of politics is equal distribution, the success of which leads to increasing production or increasing population. Just like creation is a change by itself—and also a cause of change—generation of a human being is a kind of a social change and a cause of political change. As the birth of one person in a family causes change in that family and change of the interest relationship among family members, the change of population changes society and changes the interest relationships among people in that society. The result is political change. The continuous generation of human beings causes the continuous change of society and of politics.

All beings are created by the intercourse of the Yin-Yang, and all living beings are created by the interaction of the male and female. If one knows the principles of the beginning and the end after observation, one can understand the processes of the birth and the death of human beings and the meanings of those lives. When we substitute these principles with the concept of the public and private interests, the public and private interests interact with each other and establish an agreement—a political achievement. If one knows the principle of the beginning and the end of political problems after observation, he can understand the occurrence and the solutions of those problems. In other words, the occurrence of the private interest and the public interest means an occurrence of the political problems. The process of conflict between the private and public interests and the process of making agreements between them is a political process; if the private interest and the public interest agree on a particular solution, it is a political accomplishment.

As the opposition and the friction between the Yin and Yang elements are recognized as a necessary phenomenon for creation, the opposition and the friction between private and public interests are recognized as necessary to the political process. As the pushing and pulling relationship between the Yin and Yang elements create change, the pushing and pulling between the private and public interests create political change. The private interest and the public interest are created alternately—there is a push-pull action in the process and there are conflicts and frictions in the process of making agreements or unifications. These oppositions and conflicts between the private interest and the public interest are a kind of political process and are a necessary evil in politics. The friction between private and public interests makes it possible to judge right or wrong; consequently, human society can grow.

Chi Tzu Chuan said, "Even though the way of universal motion is shown differently, the goal of the universe is same; even though the thoughts are more than hundreds, the achievement is the same." Just like the description given by Chi Tzu Chuan, political tools and the political process may be several but the ultimate aim of politics is the same. *Chou I* described, "The shrinking is for the jumping, and the bending is for the stretching. Even though they are jealous and antagonistic, their aims communicate with each other." Similarly, the public interest and the private interest are heterogeneous and antagonistic, but they are in accord with respect to the ultimate goal—creation. As the theory of change defined change as a necessary and beneficial thing, political change also is necessary and beneficial. As the assertion of the theory of change states: "When it is needed it will change; when it changes, it will go through; once it goes through, it is maintained for a long time." If politics is closed, then politics should change. When it changes, it will solve the problems; once it solves the problems, it will sustain the situation for a long time. *Chou I* insisted, "Change is a beneficial thing. The friction of love and hatred creates good luck and ill luck, and interaction of truth and false creates the gain and the loss." This principle is also applicable to political theory in that political change is a beneficial thing. The friction of the love and hate between the public interest and the private interest decides the good luck and the ill luck in political affairs, the estrangement and the closeness create good luck and ill luck in political affairs, the estrangement and the closeness create repentance and shamefulness, and the interaction of truth and falsity of the interest relationships decides the gain and the loss.

Just like "when the heaven and the earth change, the plants and the trees grow, and when the heaven and the earth close, the wise man hides," when the relationship between the public interest and the private interest changes, human society grows. And if the interaction between the two interests closes and the relationship is not changed, the wise men hide for their protection, and political affairs are stymied.

The exquisite principle of the Yin-Yang lies in its irregularity. Continuous peace causes corruption; when things are chaotic, this disorder will be recovered without fail. This principle also states the necessity of the political change. The exquisite principle of politics is in the irregular relationship between the public interest and the private interest, and is an abnormal condition. If the peaceful period continues too long, society will become corrupt. If politics is not impartial, the society will be chaotic. If society loses its order, it will be recovered inevitably. Therefore, continuous change is necessary and beneficial.

Yang Pien Yin Hua

The theory of Yang Pien Yin Hua—that when the Yang element is extreme it turns into the Yin element and when Yin element is extreme it turns into the Yang element—can be used to explain, logically, the theory of the alternate creation of Yin-Yang, but it is not possible to use it to explain the theory of flying and hiding mystery (飛伏神理論). This failure is shifted to the actions of Kuei Shen (鬼神). Therefore, when we substitute these theories with the public and private concept, it is impossible to explain logically, and results in: When the public interest is extreme it turns into the private interest and when the private interest is extreme it turns into the public interest. If creation starts with the public interest it will end at the private interest, and vice-versa. The extreme altruist or extreme egoist may be able to change their character to the opposite, or an extreme altruist or extreme egoist may contain opposite characteristics inside himself, but it is impossible to logically explain the principle of change in both cases.

Cycling Order

According to the theory of change, "There is nothing fixed and unchangeable and there is nothing that stays the same permanently; the law of nature is endless change and the continuous cycling and repetition." Politics is also the same as nature, so there is no politics that is fixed and unchangeable, there are no political states that permanently stay the same, and the theory of political change is one of endless change and of continuous cycling and repetition. This explanation sounds very reasonable because human beings repeat birth and death, so the interest relationships among humans are changing all the time and the change and movement of populations change the interest relationships among people. Urbanization and industrialization make political changes more complex and it becomes difficult to verify the cycling order and the periodicity.

There are many cycling orders in the theory of change. The theory of the alternate creation of Yin-Yang is a cycling theory, the process of the creation of the five elements according to Ho Tu (河圖) and Lo Hsu (洛書) is a cycling theory, the change of seasons is a cycling theory, the theory of the seven-step change is a cycling theory, and the theory of creation of heaven and earth of Hsiao Kang Chieh (邵康節的天地開闢論)

is a cycling theory. The Yin and Yang elements are created alternately and this cycle repeats endlessly.

As the cycle of growth—the maturity, the stand-still, the extinction—repeats in nature, the political problems which arise from the conflict between public and private interests also repeat. If the change of human society is a circulation of Yang leading to the pre-heaven period with Yin leading to a post-heaven period—like the theory of Hsiao Kang Chieh—the politics of human society might be a circulation of the public leading to a socialist society and the private leading to an individualist society. But verification of this is extremely difficult. If individualism and socialism circulate, it would seem to be possible to verify this through historical study.

The theory of change explained the general theory of circulation in these words: "There is nothing that is not tilted even if it is flat and there is nothing that is not recovered even if it is tilted. If the corruption is extreme, it will recover certainly." These general theories are applicable to political theories as: "There is no politics that is not tilted completely, even if it is impartial, and there is no politics that is not recovered if it is tilted." Even though you are in trouble, do the right thing so you will not be blamed. Even if it is tilted, don't worry—do your best in sincerity. If politics becomes corrupt extremely, it will be recovered certainly. These theories can be explained logically and can be verified in reality.

Harmonious Unification

Harmonious unification is the completion of creation by the unification of the Yin and Yang. The unification of the Yin-Yang means a birth of life and the separation of the Yin-Yang means a death. So unification is a beneficial thing, and harmonious unification is better than antagonistic separation. When these theories are substituted with the public and private interests, it becomes a political theory: The harmonious unification of the public interest and the private interest reveals the solution to the political problems. When the public and private interests unify, political problems are solved. But if the interests separate, political problems arise. Therefore, unification of the public interest and the private interest is beneficial and harmonious unification is better than the alternative.The comparison of the shape of the hexagrams described very well that harmonious unification is a good phenomenon and that discord is a bad phenomenon. The comparison of the Tai hexagram and the Pi hexagram (泰卦, 否卦), the Chien hexagram and the Sung hexagram (謙卦, 訟卦), and the Hsien hexagram and the Kuei hexagram (咸卦, 睽卦) are typical examples.

The Tai hexagram is the shape in which three heavy Yin lines go down from the top and three light Yang lines go up from the bottom, so that they meet at the middle without hindrance. Just like the Tai hexagram, if the private interest goes down from the top and the public interest goes up from the bottom, both interests meet in the middle and unify harmoniously, resulting in a solution to a political problem. On the other hand, the Pi hexagram is the shape in which three heavy Yin lines go down at the bottom and three light Yang lines go up at the top. They fail to unify and they separate. If politics resembles this shape, the public interest will go up at the top and the private interest will go down at the bottom—political problems will be worse and society will fail to make unified agreements.

In the Chien hexagram, high mountains stay under the low earth, which means modesty. The public worker who is in the king's position takes care of people and deducts from the fullness and adds to the lack, so people obey the public worker. In this case, the king subtracts some from the rich and adds some to the poor and raises people evenly. He is also modest in character, so the private interest and the public interest harmonize together. On the other hand, in the Sung hexagram the strong king suppresses the people with strong authority at the top and the people watch for the higher position at the bottom. A dispute arises, so the public interest and the private interest are hostile to each other and without unification. In this situation, because one is compelled to fight both sides will be hurt.

In the Hsien hexagram, when a man approaches a woman in a deferent manner, the woman is impressed and unifies with the man, pleasantly. Just as in the Hsien hexagram, if public workers (who represent the public interest) approach the people (who represent the private interest) in a modest posture, the people are inspired and accept the public interest. In this case the public interest and the private interest unify harmoniously—political problems are solved easily. On the other hand, in the Kuei hexagram (the water and the fire), two Yin-natured elements take both the upper and the lower positions, so they antagonistic each other and regard each other with jealousy; they cannot unify harmoniously. Therefore, in this hexagram, people who pursue private interests take their places in upper and lower positions and show antagonism and jealousy toward each other—they cannot unify and they fail to make agreement.

Chou I introduced a few models of the unification of the Yin-Yang. They are the Tai-Hsien type (泰咸型), the pure hexagram type (純卦型), the Tung Jên type (同人型), the Sui-Tsui type (隨萃型), the Chun type (屯型), and the Shih Ho type (噬嗑型).

As in the Tai Hsien hexagrams, the Tai Hsien type of unification is when the Yin and Yang elements gather together. Because the public interests and the private interests gather together, they unify harmoniously and solve the political problems in the most ideal manner. The pure hexagrams are constructed with the same trigrams—the upper trigram and lower trigram. They are Kan (乾), Kun (坤), Kán (坎), Li (離), Hsün (巽), Tui (兌), Chen (震), and Kén (艮). Because the upper and lower trigrams have the same nature, they unite. This unity is not the unification of the Yin-Yang. The public interest unites with the public interest, the private interest with the private interest, the dangerous things with the dangerous things, the passionate things with the passionate things, the moving things with the moving things, the pleasant things with the pleasant things, the blocked things with the blocked things, the wind with the wind.

Even though Tung Jên is not a pure hexagram, the upper trigram Kan and the lower trigram Li have the same upward nature. In this hexagram, because the fifth line (the king's position) is impartial, the other five lines follow the fifth line. Therefore, when public workers apply impartial policies all the people unify and the public and private interests unify.

In the Sui hexagram, when the lower trigram (Yang) moves, the upper trigram (Yin) complies with Yang pleasantly, and the Yin and Yang unify without hindrance. In this type the public interest follows the private interest and private interests comply with public interests, without rejection, so they accomplish unification and successfully make political agreements. Even though the way that the public interest follows the private interest is a unilateral following, because the private interest complies with the public interest it is a kind of the harmonious unification.

The Tsui type is related to the spirit of the public man. If the governor who is at the king's position maintains the medium and justice (中正) and governs the people with virtue, people gather around him and happily follow him. This type is typical of the harmonious union of the public and private interests. When public workers carry out their public duty righteously, individuals will cooperate with public affairs and pursue own interests together (公私和合).

The Chun type is a unification of the Yin and the Yang, although there are some hindrances of the Yin lines to the process of unification. This type breaks through the hindrances and unifies, but not without some difficulties. In the Chun hexagram (屯卦), the public interest (first line) attempts to unify with the private interest (fourth line), but meets the hindrance of the Yin lines in the middle. The public interest moves through this dangerous situation, breaks through the difficulties, and, in the end, meets the private interest. This is not a harmonious unification but is a kind of unification of the Yin and Yang, and can reach political goals.

The Shi Ho type is a noisy unification. Thunder and lightning combine and unify through mastication, so everything goes well. This type helps people through the administration of justice by the thunder's authority and the lightning's judgment. In this type of unification, the private interest and the public interest unify through a rough-and-tumble process that decides right or wrong through trial and error and decides reward and punishment through judgment. Shih Ho is not harmonious unification; it is a unification of the private and public interests through noisy friction and bears political fruit. This is very similar to the democratic political process which finds the public interest through the friction among private interests, and which helps private individuals through the application of public policy. Chou I introduced the modesty (謙), the public way (大道), the medium and the justice (中正), and the virtuous politics (德治) as means of harmonious unifications. In the Chien (謙卦) and Hsien hexagrams (咸卦), Yang approaches Yin with modesty, and deducts some from excess and adds some to lack, so Yang inspires Yin and unifies harmoniously. When this theory is substituted with political concepts, the public workers who carry out the public duties modestly approach the people who pursue private interests and deduct some things from any found excesses and give some to the more unfortunate people, thus inspiring people to cooperate with public affairs. Therefore, Chien is a way that public workers should follow in order to achieve harmonious unification of the private and public interests.

The Ta Tao (大道) is a public way to facilitate harmonious unification between public and private interests. The Ta Tao of the Great Learning (大學) is a spirit of the public way which enhances four of the original virtues—the humanity (仁), the righteousness (義), the courtesy (禮), and the wisdom (智)—and trains the body in preparation to maintain the state of pure virtue. It applies the truly impartial policies to the people and is inspiring to them. The Ta Tao of the *Book of Courtesy* (禮記) is a similar spirit of the public way which respects others as one respects his relatives, gives duties to youths, adults, and the elderly, permits the widow, the widower, the solitudes, and sick persons a place to recuperate and train, and constructs a society of mutual aid. Similarly, if the public workers who carry out the public duty are really impartial, people will follow the public interest. And if they help the old, sick, or weak person, and raise the people evenly, people will be inspired and trustingly follow the public way. Because the subject of politics is one of pursuing the public interest, if public workers follow the public way like this, all the people will unite with public workers and make a harmonious unification of the public and private interests. Therefore, the Ta Tao is an ideal way to achieve the harmonious unification of the public interest and the private interest.

The medium and justice (中正) is a way of harmonious unification which has three different parts—the middle line (中道), the neutralization or moderation (中和), and the righteousness (貞). The middle line that is defined in the *Book of Moderation* means a balanced position— not too much and not too little. The middle line has no true character; its character changes depending on the time and place. The middle line is not a norm of good or bad and is not a standard of truth or false. The middle line is just a middle line that a wise man cannot follow because he is too wise and that a foolish man cannot follow because he is too foolish. The middle line is an important way of harmonious unification. It is the most common method that gives the greatest satisfaction for the greatest population. When individuals who each pursue their best interests fail to agree and struggle with each other, a governor may determine the extreme points of both sides and take the middle ground and apply this medium to them. This middle line may not be a good one or may not be a just one, but it is one method of harmonious unification that insures the greatest satisfaction for the greatest population. This might be a general rule of modern liberal democracy.

Moderation is a way of mental training and a moral philosophy for saint training. When one enhances the four original virtues and maintains the state of pure virtue, he will not express any feelings such as gladness, anger, grief, or pleasure. This is the state of medium (中). Even though he express these feelings, if he maintains control of them, he is in the state of moderation (和). The doctrine of the medium and moderation (中和的道) is that human feelings are not expressed at all or that human feelings are controlled by virtue, even though feelings are expressed. If all the members of society maintain the state of medium or moderation, society will harmonize and realize the complete unity of public and private interests. If only public workers maintain this state of medium or moderation, they will serve the people by implementing impartial policies, accomplishing harmonious unification of the public and private interests.

The righteousness (貞) means right, straight, or just, and it involves correct behavior, correct position, and/or several other kinds of righteousness. It includes the value of naturalism, the value of medium, and the value of the harmonious unification. Public workers have proper actions as public workers and private individuals have proper behaviors as private individuals. When public workers and private workers do the right things, they will unify harmoniously.

The virtuous politics (德) usually means a generous govern-ing by a monarch. The virtuous way in which a king governs the people is a method of harmonious unification of the public and private interests. This virtue includes the humanity, the righteousness, the courtesy, and the wisdom, but the virtuous politics has an emphasis on the humanity. When a king applies the proper guidance rather than punishment, takes the lead rather than succumbing to pressure, and puts the courtesy before authority, people are inspired, refrain the evil-doing, and cooperate in public affairs. Therefore, the virtuous politics achieves harmonious unification of the public interest and the private interest, and political problems are solved automatically. In general, the virtuous politics is a kind of the governance of the king. Because it is a way to inspire people and to lead people toward virtuous behavior, it is a way of harmonious unification between public and private interests. So in this situation, private individuals become involved in public affairs by themselves.

After substituting the concept of the public interest and the private interest into the theory of the harmonious unification, and generalizing and establishing the political theories from that, it transforms into an almost perfect political theory. The value of harmonious unification, the method of harmonious unification, and the type of the harmonious unification were theorized.

There are also disharmonious unifications of the interests. Unifications through conquest are shown in the Li hexagram (離卦), Kuei hexagram (夬卦), Ko hexagram (革卦), and Chien hexagram (謙卦), and there were discordant unifications in the Chun (屯卦) and Shi Ho hexagrams (噬嗑卦).

Balance

Even though the theory of change expressed clearly the Thought of the Noble Yang and Ignoble Yin (大貴小賤思想) and the Thought of the Support Yang and Suppress Yin (扶陽抑陰思想), it explained that the Yin-Yang has equal value in creation. Yin-Yang exists together all the time and it is almost impossible to consider them separately. Because creation is possible only by the unification of the Yin-Yang, it has the same value in the creation. When the Yin element and the Yang element unify with equal strengths of elements, the outcome is superior to unbalanced unification.

When we substitute these thoughts with the concept of the public interest and the private interest, the outcome is as follows. "The lonesome public interest cannot start the creation and isolated private interest cannot complete the creation. So if the public interest is there, the private interest is there, too, and if the private interest is there, the public interest should follow it (魂魄說). The private interest should follow the public interest. That is the principle of the co-reaction of the Yin-Yang (隨卦). If the private interest leads it will lose the way, but if it follows it will take advantage. If the private interest becomes prosperous and engages in public affairs, it will surely fight with the public interest and both will bleed all over the field because she confuses the situation that there is no public interest around (坤卦)." When the public interest changes to the private interest, it is not a growing period, but a withering period. When the private interest turns to the public interest it means growing. Therefore, *Chou I* treated the public interest as noble and the private interest as ignoble (蔡氏四十九耆虛一體數圖解說). The Thought of Noble Yang and Ignoble Yin (大貴小賤思想) is expressed very well in the comparison of the next hexagrams: Kou and Fu (姤卦，復卦); Tun and Lin (遯卦，臨卦); Pi and Tai (否卦，泰卦); Kuan and Ta Chuang (觀卦，大壯卦); and Po and Kuai (剝卦，夬卦).

The Kou hexagram is the time period when private interest begins to grow, so it is the time of the beginning of declining. Fu is the period when the public interest starts to grow, so it explains that a decadent period is going and that a vivid period is coming. In the Tun hexagram the public interest is declining and the private interest is growing, so one should avoid the danger. The private interest is growing and the public interest is declining in the Pi hexagram, so the public man hides and the private man is triumphant. On the other hand, the public interest is growing and the private interest is declining in the Tai hexagram, so the public interest and the private interest unify harmoniously and everything goes well. In the Kuai period, because the private man who pursues the private interest is above several public men, society will become light and good by repulsing private interest.

The theory of change insisted that the public interest takes priority over the private interest and that the public man has priority over the private man in the relationship between them, but it prefers the balanced shape of the public interest and the private interest. *Chou I* defined the excess of the public interest or the excess of the private interest as bad phenomena. When the public interest is excessive, the excessive duties make the girder bend and heavy things sink in the water, so the sound rings loud but nothing can really be accomplished. When the private interest is excessive, the small matters—private affairs—can be achieved but the large public affairs cannot be achieved. In this situation, the public man falls into trouble by mischief of the private interest; unification of the public interests and the private interests fail.

The Po hexagram (剝卦) where the private interest pushes out the public interest or the Kuei hexagram (夬卦) where the public interest pushes out the private interest are also not recommendable phenomena. In this situation, threats and intimidation are common and a lawsuit arises frequently, thus the struggle continues.

When the balance theory of *Chou I* is alternately used as a political theory, it provides a few political principles. One principle is that the public interest takes priority over the private interest and that the public interest should lead the private interest. The private interest cannot lead the public interest in the relationship between the public interest and the private interest nor in the relationship between the public man and the private man. Even though the public interest has priority over the private interest, the public interest should not be excessive. If the public interest expresses itself excessively and the private interest is ignored, a loud, noisy sound is heard but there will be no political fruit. If the private interest expresses itself excessively and the public interest is ignored, only small accomplishments are possible. Therefore, the theory of change suggests that the unification of the public and private interests under a balanced condition is the best situation.

Stability

The theory of change is a principle of change. It praises the change and it emphasizes the theory of change and the process of change, but it also emphasizes the necessity of stability. The concept of the stability of *Chou I* has two meanings. The first concept is that change can occur according to certain changing principles, so this principle of change should not change. The second concept is that the Yin and Yang have different natures and different functions, so the Yin and Yang should do the right functions in the right places. When we alternate this theory of stability to political theory, the outcome is as explained below.

The origination of political problems lies in the origination of the public interests and the private interests, and the solution to political problems is the unification of the public and private interests; the repetition of the circulation of the origin and the solution occur according to certain principles and this principle should not change. So political change can occur orderly and normal creation is possible. The normal function is a unification of the private interest and the public interest. If the political change is not the correct change, and if the accidental change (irregular happening) occurs frequently, the political function will not be stable and it will be difficult to accomplish political goals.

The theory of stability—that both the public interest and the private interest should do their right duties in correct positions—is well described in the Hêng hexagram (恒卦) and the Chia Jên hexagram (家人卦). In the Hêng hexagram, the public worker who pursues the public interest takes the upper position and the private worker who pursues the private interest takes the lower position. That a private man takes the humble posture at the lower position is normal in the relationship between the public worker and the private worker. The public worker devotes himself to public duty at the right position and the private workers devotes himself to private duty at the right position. This relationship can prolong good periods.

The political fruit can be reaped by the unification of the public interest and the private interest, but once the position and the duty is determined, the public workers and the private workers should devote their best to their position in order to create the best result. Similarly, even though the marriage of man and woman can create the second generation, the married man and woman should do their right duties in their right position, and when the woman takes the humble posture toward husband, their relationship is prolonged for a long time.

In the structure of the hexagram, each line has responding line. When corresponding lines are constructed with a Yin line and a Yang line, it is a correct response. When the second line is a Yin line and the fifth line is a Yang line, it is the most righteous response—called Chung Cheng (中正). When the first, third, and fifth lines are Yang lines, and second, fourth, and sixth lines are Yin lines, this hexagram means completion and is called Chi Chi (既濟卦).

Just as in the structure of the hexagram of *Chou I*, if the corresponding positions are constructed with the private interest and the public interest in the political structure, it would be the right response. If the public interest responds to the public interest, there will be no harmonious unification, and if the private interest responds to the private interest, then jealousy and antagonism will make for continuous discord. The political structure is better if it has the structure of Chia Jên. In the Chia Jên hexagram, all the family members—father, son, elder brother, younger brother, husband, and wife—do their right duties in the right position. As in the Chia Jên hexagram, if all the components of the government—emperor, king, subject, minister, bureaucrats, and people—do their correct duties in the right position, the government will maintain normal function for a long time and will grow under the stability. When the theory of the stability of *Chou I* is alternated with political theory, it becomes a system theory. In order to carry out the orderly creation through the continuous unification of the public interest and the private interest, the government should be institutionalized. The relationship between the public and private interests should be defined and the duties of each position should be determined by regulation. Therefore, when all the components of the government do their proper duties in the right positions, the government will grow under the stable system. The king does his public duties at the highest position and maintains the order, the subjects (public workers) support the king and take care of the people between the king and the people, and the people carry out their private goals under the public workers. Thus, the continuous unification of the public interest and the private interest is possible.

The Theory of Change as a Theory of Political Change

The subject of this thesis is the development of the theory of political change by alternating the changing theory of nature to the changing theory of society. So the first question is whether the theories of natural change can be applicable or not to the theories of social change, and the second question is whether the theories of social change can be applicable to the theories of political change. *Chou I* answered to this question by itself in explaining not only the process of creation from Tai Chi to extinction, but also the theory of human relationships and the value assertion; that is, a judgment of the right or wrong of a particular event or behavior.

In the explanation of the hexagrams, *Chou I* substituted the Yin line and the Yang line for the female and the male, and for the private man and the public man. *Chou I* also substituted each line of the hexagrams for the political positions—such as the king's position, subject's position, peoples' position, etc. This thesis chased the concept of Ta Hsiao (大小) and found out that the concept of Ta means the Yang and public affairs, while the concept of Hsiao means the Yin and private affairs. When the Yang means public and the Yin means private, the relationship of the Yin-Yang is the relationship between the public interest and the private interest, the relationship between the public man and the private man, and the relationship between socialism and individualism—the Yin-Yang relationship turns out to be at the core of politics. It becomes possible to extract the theory of political change from the theory of change. But because the change of nature and the change of politics are different in nature, we cannot alternate all the theories of change with political theories. Therefore, all the theories should be examined to see if such substitution is warranted. The next analysis is an examination of the possibility of doing so.

Toegae's theory of original natures and human feelings (性情論), which explained the origination of the public mind (公心) and the private mind (私心) on an individual level, was a metaphysical theory, so this theory is impossible to verify. Toegae's theory that the private mind (人心) and the public mind (道心) are competing inside the human mind is possible to verify in reality. Togae's theory that five original natures (仁, 義, 禮, 智, 信) arise from the five elements of strength

(木, 金, 火, 水, 土)—heaven-given natures (天性)—and that seven passions (喜, 怒, 哀, 懼, 愛, 惡, 慾) arise from the human body—body-given natures (人情)—remains as a subject of future study.

There is no way to verify the circulation theory that the public element of strength and the private element of strength arise alternately, but it is possible to verify the theory that the public interest contains the private interest and that the private interest contains the public interest. And it is possible to verify the theory that a social interest is a combined union of several private interests and several public interests. The expansion and diminution phenomenon (盈虛消息現象) of the public interest and the private interest may be possible to apply in reality. The theory that the public interest and the private interest are heterogeneous, and are conflicting but have same origin, can be verified. When the conflicting relationship of the Yin-Yang is substituted with the conflicting relationship of the private interest and the public interest, it becomes a core of politics and turns into a perfect theory of politics. The theory that even though the private interest and the public interest oppose and conflict with each other, that this relationship is not a reciprocally negating struggle but is a process of seeking agreement that it is a mutually assisting relationship, a mutually infiltrating relation, and a perpetually circulating process, becomes a perfect theory of politics.

It is also a perfect political theory that the goal of politics is the creation and the growth of human society through the unification of the private interest and the public interest, that the creation is a change by itself and the cause of change, that the origination of the public interest and the private interest is the origination of the political problem, and that the seeking of agreement between the private and public interests through the conflicting process is the political solution.

The theory of Yang Pien Yin Hua—that when the public interest is extreme it becomes the private interest and when the private interest is extreme it becomes public interest—is impossible to verify or to explain logically. This theory is not possible to verify by human ability, so it was turned into Kuei Shen (鬼神).

The theory of circulation—that nothing is fixed and unchangeable and the laws of nature are endlessly changing in a continuous, repetitious cycle—is somewhat logical, but it is difficult to treat it as a reasonable theory until the periodicity becomes clear.

The theory that there is no politics which does not tilt (no matter how impartial) and that there is no politics which does not recover if it is tilted is logical and is possible to verify in reality.

The theory of the harmonious unification of the private interest and the public interest is more important as a theory for value assertion than as a theory of change. Recognizing the value of harmonious unification, and developing the model and the method of the harmonious unification of the private and public interests, is very helpful for the study of political development. If the ideal model and the ideal method of the harmonious unification are developed, it would be a goal of the voluntary pursuance by human will.

The balance theory—that balanced unification of the private interest and the public interest achieves the greater political fruit—is also a theory for value claim rather than a theory of change. Balance theory has a basic value problem that is contrary to the Thought of Support Yang and Suppress Yin (扶陽抑陰思想) and the Public Prior Thought (公利優先思想) of *Chou I*. These two thoughts insist upon the priority of the public interest in the relationship between the public interest and the private interest, and the balance theory insists on equality and balance in the interrelation between them. This subject is related to the stability, efficiency, and effectiveness of the system. Modern political systems attempt to solve this problem by separation of the private and public sectors. In any event, the contrary view of the Public-Prior Thought and Balance Thought remains a central question in the political field for future study. The theory of stability and the theory of change have opposite meanings. According to the theory of stability, the principle of the change should not change, and the duties and functions of the public workers and the private workers should not change. Therefore, the theory of stability is a kind of system theory that emphasizes orderly change under a stable system. This theory suggests many questions about the causes and the necessities of system change, and the limitations and the necessities of system stability.

When we alternate the theory of change with the theory of political change, we could establish a particular theory system that is different from the existing theories and that can reinforce the existing theories. Existing theories have determined the conflict between conservatives and reformists or the struggle between classes as causes of political change. On the other hand, the theory of change determined the conflict between the public interest and the private interest as causes of political change.

So the theory of change focuses on the origination of the public interest and private interest, on the unification and the dispersion of them, and on the opposition and the conflict among them. The reason why the theory of change is more perfect than other theories is that no matter whether the conflicts and the contradictions arise between conservatives and reformists or between the classes, all the causes of the conflict belong to the public interests or the private interests.

Secondly, the theory of change is the same as the dialectics from the point of view that competition and struggle are essential factors for change. But the relationship in the theory of change is not a mutually negating one, or of utmost opposition; rather, this conflicting phenomenon is a process of seeking agreement and is a reciprocally supporting relationship.

The theory of change is different from other conflict theories because it seeks political fruit through the unification of the public interest and the private interest. Because the other conflict theories are the mutually negating relationships, they create political fruit by the repulsion of the opposition. Therefore, the political fruit should be an excessive public interest phenomenon or an excessive private interest phenomenon.

Notes

1. Kim, Hyuck Jae 金赫濟, 原本集註 周易, 明文堂, ibid. p. 78. p.83. p.161. p.337. p. 359.

2. Kim, Hyuck Jae, ibid. p. 424-427.
   金赫濟, 上同, pp.424~427. "乾은 健也이오 坤은 順也이오"(第七章), "乾爲首이오 坤爲腹이오"(第九章). "乾은 天也이라 故로 稱乎父이오 坤은 地也이라 故로 稱乎母이오"(第十章), "乾은 爲天爲圜, 爲君, 爲父, 爲玉, 爲金, 爲寒, 爲氷, 爲大赤, 爲良馬, 爲老馬, 爲瘠馬, 爲駁馬, 爲木果", "坤爲地 爲母, 爲布, 爲釜, 爲吝嗇, 爲均, 爲子母牛, 爲大輿, 爲文, 爲衆, 爲柄, 其於地也, 爲黑"

3. Sim, Jong Chuel
   沈鍾哲, 周易, 大韓曆法研究所, 乾爲天卦, 五爻爻辭, p.34. "夫大人者는 與天地合其德하며 與日月合其明하며 與四時合其序하며 與鬼神合其吉凶하며 先天而天弗違하며 後天而奉天時하나니 天且弗違온 而況於人乎이며 況於鬼神乎이여"

4. Kim, Hyuck Jae,
   金赫濟, 大學中庸, 明文堂, p.9 : "程子曰親, 當作新, ○. 大學者, 大人之學也, 明, 明之也, 明德者, 人之所得乎天, 而虛靈不昧, 以具衆理, 以應萬事者也, 爲氣稟所拘, 人欲所蔽, 則有時而昏, 然, 其本體之明則有當息者, 故學者, 當因其所發而遂明之, 以復其初也. 新者, 革其舊之謂也, 言, 旣自明其明德, 又當推以及人, 使之亦有以去 其舊染之汚也, 止者, 必至於是, 而不遷之意, 至善則事理當然之極也, 必其有以盡夫 天理之極, 而無一毫 人欲之私也. ○. 新安吳氏曰 ⋯ 止至善爲明明德 新民之標的極盡 天理絶無 人欲爲止至善 ⋯. ○. 新安陳氏曰 天理人欲相爲消長幾 有一毫 人欲之使 不能盡夫天理之極 不得云止於至善矣.

5. Sim, Jong Chuel, ibid. p. 89-90.
   沈鍾哲, 上同, pp.89~90, "象曰謙亨은 天道가 下濟而光明하고 地道卑而上行이라 天道는 虧盈而益謙하고 地道는 變盈而流謙하고 鬼神은 害盈而福謙하고 人道는 惡盈而好謙하나니 謙은 尊而光하고 卑而不可踰이니 君子之終이라"

6. 禮記의 大同章, "大道之行也 天下爲公選賢與能 講信修睦, 故人不獨親其親 不獨子己子, 使老有所終, 壯有所用 幼有所長, 矜寡孤獨廢疾者 皆有所養, 男有分女, 有歸貨惡其於地也, 不必藏, 於己力惡其不出 於身也, 不必爲己, 是故 謀閉而不興, 盜竊亂賊而不作, 外戶而不閉 是謂大同"

7. Sim, Jong Chuel, ibid. p. 36.
   沈鍾哲, 上同, p.36, "象曰 至哉라 坤元이여 萬物이 資生하나니 乃順承天이여 坤厚載物이 德合无疆하며 含弘光大하여 物品이 咸亨하나니라. 牝馬는 地類이니 行地无疆하며 柔順利貞이 君子攸行이라. 先하면 迷하여 失道하고 後하면 順하여 得常하리니 西南得朋은 乃與類行이요 東北喪朋은 乃終有慶하리니 安貞之吉이 應地无疆이니라."

8. Lee, Sang Eun, 李相殷, 聖學十圖譯解, 서울 : 退溪學研究院, p.47.
   Lee, Sang Eun,
   李相殷, 退溪의 生涯와 學問, 서울 : 退溪學研究院. 이외에도 四・七論爭에 관한 硏究는 많이 있다.

9. Kim, Hyuck Jae, 金赫濟, 大學中庸, 上同, p.9.

Chapter 5

Search for the Pattern of the Political Change

The Meanings of Searching New Theory

Previous chapters summarized the theories of change in *Chou I*, alternated those with the political theories, and examined the applicability of those theories to real society. The remaining subject is to find a worthy model of political change and working that model into a new theory of political change. As in previous analyses, there are very few avenues which humans can pursue concerning the process of change. Nature changes according to the laws of nature. Therefore, man's way is simply following the laws of nature. But there are assertions that present human society is not changing according to those laws. Some have asserted that original human beings were free and equal but that current human beings are unequal and chained. Others say original human beings lived in competitive circumstances where the weak fell prey to the strong but that the artificial suppression of competition has disturbed the development of present human society. All of these assertions are possible, if one accepts the premise of that humans have the ability and the right to decide their fate.

If human beings have the ability and freedom to decide the fate of their race, humans cannot leave their fate to the laws of nature—human beings should develop their own fate. In order to do that, humans should determine the relationship between themselves and the relationship between themselves and nature; they should then decide the correct course to pursue. According to *Chou I*, human beings have the right and ability to decide their own fate. But if a person follows the laws of nature he will be successful; however, if he goes against the laws of nature he will perish. Therefore, in order to correct the wrong actions the saint who has a thorough knowledge of nature should come out and lead the human race down the right path.

This assertion of *Chou I* has two meanings. First, human beings have freedom to go against the laws of nature. Second, a human being who knows the natural laws thoroughly can correct the wrong things in human society. Therefore, humans should put forth a sincere effort toward correcting human society. So it becomes logical that human beings can find the right type of political change which will fit within the laws of nature and can enable them to politically rule in the right way.

Modern political society has several contradictions. Some people are dying from hunger and armed disputes have killed many. But there is no mutually agreed upon rule of distribution of resources and political power; there is no universal agreement on the goals and methods of politics. Seeking the political pattern which is possible to pursue from the theory of change should be a reasonable goal of modern political students.

The last chapter of this thesis searches for the most reasonable pattern of political change among the political theories extracted from the theory of change and examines the applicability of that theory to the real world. Even though the utility of the theory is limited, and while it is difficult to create a suitable environment for this pattern, political students should follow the direction of the *Chou I*: "If you seek sincerely it will show you the way, if you try sincerely you will achieve it—just do your best, why worry?"

Definition of the BHUPP (Ta Hsiao Chun Ho, 大小均合)

When we generalize the theory of change, the ultimate goal of nature is creation and the goal of human beings, as a part of nature, is also creation. Creation is achieved by the unification of the Yin element and the Yang element; those arise from Tai Chi. When the Yin-Yang relationship is converted to political relationships, it becomes one between the private interest and the public interest. The private and public interests arise continuously from human beings who are a kind of Tai Chi. Through the process of separation, unification, dispersion, and gathering, the private interests and the public interests create the complicated interest relationships. Because politics is a matter of interest, the complicated interest relationships create the complicated political problems.

As Yin and Yang oppose and conflict with each other when they arise but carry out creation by unification, the private interest and the public interest oppose and conflict with each other at the start but carry out creation by unification. Therefore, the origination of the public interest and the private interest is an origination of political problems and the unification of the private interest and the public interest is a solution to the political problem. The more complicated the interest relationship between the private interest and the public interest, the more complicated the political problem—and the more difficult the solution is to find. The relationship between private and public can be one among individuals or an interrelation among groups or nations. The object of politics is not the creation of political problems but the solution to them, so the goal of politics is seeking an accord point between the private interest and the public interest. The unification of the private and public interests at the accorded point is called the unification of the private interest and the public interest. (大小結合).

There are many types of unification of the private interest and the public interest. In the Sui type, when the public interest moves, the private interest follows pleasantly and unifies; in the Tsui type, because the public interest takes the middle position and carries out impartial policies, the private interest joins the public. In the Tung Jen type, the private interest and the public interest unify their actions in the same direction; in the Shih Ho type, the private interest and the public interest unify through the noisy and painful process of friction. In the Chun type, the private interest and the public interest overcome the dangerous obstacles and ultimately unify; in the Tai-Hsien type, the private interest and the public interest take positions which they then move toward each other, thus unifying harmoniously. The noble and prior and light public interest approaches the upper private interest from a lower position with a humble posture, while the ignoble and heavy private interest moves down from the upper position. They meet in the middle and unify pleasantly without any resistance. This kind of unification is called the harmonious unification of the private interest and the public interest (大小和合).

There are many types of harmonious unifications between the private interest and the public interest. The great public interest can unify with the great private interest, the great public interest can unify with the small private interest, the small public interest can unify with the great private interest and the small public interest can unify with the small private interest. In these cases, unification between the same sizes of the interests results in greater accomplishments than unification between interests of different sizes. When the sizes of the public and private interests are similar, unification is easier to achieve. This kind of unification is called a balanced harmonious unification of the private interest and the public interest (大小均合).When human society fails to grow normally or when society meets with political difficulties, the best conscious solution is to lead society to the balanced harmonious unification of the private interest and the public interest (BHUPP). The BHUPP completes creation by leading to unification of the private interest and the public interest. Because there is no resistance, they unify pleasantly and the process is harmonious; because the private interest and the public interest are, in effect, of equal strength, the fruit is great. Therefore, the BHUPP is the most reasonable pattern of political change and is the most developed way of managing politics. If one can change the relationship between the public interest and the private interest to the state of the BHUPP and if one can maintain the state of the BHUPP, he can accomplish normal growth for human society—a goal human beings have a duty for which to sincerely strive.

But according to the theory of change, it is unusual for humans to change the political environment to the state of the BHUPP. Numerous humans bear and die endlessly and natural disasters and diseases disturb orderly change. The increase of population changes the interest relationships among people concerning the rights to use particular materials and concerning property ownership. Many times, the increase causes the dispute. Because of the complicated relationships of the interests, it is very difficult to take the political situation to the state of the BHUPP; even if the political environment makes it to the state of the BHUPP, it is difficult to maintain that state because the situation changes immediately after the unification. Because human beings live in an environment that changes continuously and repeats the cycling order, *Chou I* recommended people to do their best according to their times and environment.

This is a limitation with the application of human will and is the difficulty the student of *Chou I* faces. Even with this limitation, the study of the BHUPP is still necessary because human beings behave by their will, regardless of the theory of change. They believe human beings have autonomy. Therefore, if their behavior is in accord with nature they will be alright. But if their behavior is against the laws of nature, someone should correct them because that is one of our nature-given duties.

Conflict Theory and the BHUPP

The dialectical theory of Hegel, with the famous Norm-Opposition-Union, is very similar to the Yin-Yang theory of *Chou I*, and there is some supposition that Hegel cited the theory of change in his theory building. The dialectical theory of Hegel has one great difference from the dialectical theory of *Chou I:* The dialectical school of Hegel treated the theory of change as a theory of development, so they defined the direction of the development and the final goals of social development. Because they determined final society as an ideal society, they applied human will in order to quickly arrive at the ideal society.

According to Hegel, there will be no war among nations in Christian European society because it is the most developed society. On the other hand, war can arise in underdeveloped societies. In fact, he asserted that war among underdeveloped societies is inevitable in order for those societies to develop. Karl Marx, who followed Hegel's dialectics, also defined the communist society as a final ideal society and introduced the developmental theory that requires the inevitable struggles in the process of development. This dialectical developmental theory operated under three premised theories. The first premise is that continuous development brings the society to an ideal state. The second premise is that the ideal society has no conflict or struggle and that the dialectical process (Thesis-Antithesis-Synthesis) stops. So if the society becomes an ideal society once, it can maintain the peaceful conditions without the dialectical conflict of Thesis-Antithesis-Synthesis. The third premise is that one must accelerate the dialectical process in order to quickly bring about the ideal society and that conflict and struggle are inevitable in the process. Therefore, they will struggle (or war) in their development.

The theory of change is a kind of dialectical theory and recognizes social development. But it is different from the previously-mentioned dialectical development theory. Chou I is the theory of change and is a kind of dialectical theory that recognizes the inevitable conflict of the Yin element and the Yang element in the process of change, but does not define the final goal of society. There is no ideal society that does not have conflict or struggle, or that stops the dialectical function of the Yin-Yang. There is only the repetition of the process of creation in the theory of change. Therefore, the value claim of the right change is possible, but the value claim of quick change is impossible to assert in the theory of change.

There are two different concepts of development in the theory of change. According to the Right Change School, Chou I is a theory of the pre-heaven period, so the growth of human society through the Yin-Yang action means a development. The Right Change School recognizes the unification function of the post-heaven period, but they recognize only cycling order, not development. So they have only an endless process of the repetition of dispersion and unification.

The other difference of Chou I from the dialectical developmental theory is that the theory of change is a theory of harmony. In the theory of change, the Yin element and the Yang element oppose and conflict in the process of origination but this conflict is not a mutually-negating struggle because their ultimate goal is creation through the unification of Yin and Yang. Therefore, Chou I dissuaded the struggle and recommended harmonious unification. Chou I recognizes occasional conquest action as a means of correcting wrong behavior, but not as an inevitable process. The unification of Yin and Yang is regarded as a reasonable phenomenon, but the conflict and the separation of Yin-Yang is not treated as such. So the theory of change is a thought of the harmonious unification.

The differences between the dialectical developmental theory and the theory of change hint at a few important points in the analysis of political realities. First, Chou I negates justification of the struggle for development in the dialectical developmental theory. War is not inevitable for human prosperity; rather, it is an obstacle to human prosperity. Chou I recognizes only the struggle that corrects the wrong actions. Chou I recognizes creation through the unification of the private interest and the public interest and it does not recognize the prosperity of one human society at the expense of another human society. Therefore, Chou I denies war or coercive rule that the evolutionist or developmental theorists justify by reason of underdevelopment. Second, the theory of the BHUPP simplifies political problems as a conflict between the private interest and the public interest. Whether the conflict is between conservatives and reformists or among classes or factions, all the conflicts can be analyzed as a simplified relationship between the private interest and the public interest. The conflict between conservatives and reformists is the conflict between the vested interest and challenger's interest. Requesting equality communicates to the public a way to rear all human beings under heaven evenly, so it is a public interest; the maintaining of a vested interest is a private interest. If the reformists attempt to take away the vested interest from the conservatives, this relationship might be a conflict between the private interest and the private interest. But if the progressives oppose the vested interests by requiring equality, this relationship might be a conflict between the private interest and the public interest. Class struggle also can be analyzed as a conflict between the private interest and the public interest because the classes become both the vested interest and the challenger's interest. Almost all of the interest relationships can be explained as relationships between private and public interests.

If the essences of conflict are determined as between a private interest and a public interest, one can find the accorded point (agreement) between the private interest and the public interest and can make a peaceful resolution rather than violent resolution.

Ideological Conflict and the BHUPP

The theory of the BHUPP very clearly explains the conflict between totalitarianism and individualism. Totalitarianism is a thought that puts priority on society. According to socialists, the ultimate goal of human beings is the prosperity of the whole human race, and a person is a part of society. So if a society does well, individuals in that society will do well, too. On the other hand, individualism prioritizes the individual. According to individualists, an individual has an ultimate goal and society has no goal. Society is constructed by individuals, so if each individual does well, then society will automatically do well. Totalitarians think that society can control the individuals' behaviors which are against social goals and that society can compel individuals to sacrifice for society. They define an egoistic mind as a vice and define a person who does not have a private mind (only a public mind) as a good person—they attempt to reconstruct the person without an egoistic mind. They try to abolish private ownership, which they view as the root of all evil, in order to create an equal and peaceful society.

Individualists insist that an individual has the right to decide his own fate and to try to maximize private freedoms. They regard the natural principle of the struggle for existence as a truth and regard free competition among people as a necessary condition for social development. They insist that the state should allow individuals the maximum freedom to compete—the only role of state is to serve as a fair referee. They define the egoistic and competitive mind as a virtue and the martyring of oneself as a vice. Therefore, they try to encourage a competitive spirit during childhood and to make their children into strong competitors.

But both extreme totalitarians and extreme individualists show many weak points. The extreme totalitarians owned the productive measures publicly and abolished private ownership. As a result, the price of individual diligence was not credited adequately; individuals became lazy, and the growth of the whole society was delayed. On the other hand, the accumulation of the result of diligence increases the gap between the rich and the poor in the individualist society. Because the accumulated wealth perpetuates the imbalance, it disturbs even growth of the human race and the social imbalance fosters violent ways of interest-seeking. In any event, totalitarians have failed to reconstruct the unselfish human mind and individualists have failed to create the human mind which is same as the wild life. The worst result came from the conflict between totalitarian society and individualist society. The totalitarians isolated their society in order to protect it from the spread of individualism and to immerse their people in totalitarianism, and the individuals isolated their society from the totalitarian society in order to protect their society from the spread of totalitarianism and to immerse their people in liberalism. The ideological disputes developed into the Cold War, divided many states, and wasted resources.

The conflict between the totalitarianism and individualism is a typical example of the conflict between the public interest and the private interest. Because totalitarianism is thought of as the public interest and individualism is thought of as the private interest, the relationship between totalitarianism and individualism is the same as the relationship between the private and public interests. As the unification of the private interest and the public interest complete creation, the unification of socialism and liberalism accomplish proper growth of human society. But the extremists commit a error that is against nature. According to the theory of change, private interest and public interest arise alternately, and the private interest contains the public interest and the public interest contains the private interest. When they unify together the goal is finally achieved—both the private interest and the public interest are equally important.

Because extremists ignore this principle, the result is predictable. The excessive public interest phenomenon (大過現象) is shown in the totalitarian society which applies the public interest too much, and the excessive private interest phenomenon (小過現象) is shown in the individualist society which applies the private interest too much. Just like in the Ta Kuo hexagram (大過卦), there is a noisy slogan of the Earthly Heaven, but the actual growth becomes slower in extreme totalitarian societies because the society lacks the sincere effort of individuals acting for their own interest. On the other hand, just as in the Hsiao Kuo hexagram (小過卦), there is some accomplishment regarding private affairs but there are difficulties concerning public affairs in extreme individual societies—poor people find it difficult to improve their condition and too much freedom hinders execution of public policy.

In addition, both sides become more extreme—they move further from each other and fail to unify, leading to more disputes. If we explain this phenomenon according to Chou I, the result is the worst one. Chou I suggested the BHUPP in order to solve the conflict between totalitarianism and individualism. The appearance of totalitarianism and individualism, and their opposition and the conflict between them, are natural phenomenon and are not abnormal. Because both socialism and liberalism are necessary lines of thought in order for the human race to reach prosperity, their appearance is a virtue, not a vice. Only the reciprocal negation is an unreasonable thing. If humans have to pursue something with great will, it is the unification of socialism and liberalism. The reciprocal negation is not productive and it is not a solution. When they recognize each other and reach an accord, problems will be solved and human society will grow. If the process is harmonious, it is a harmonious unification; if the private interest and the public interest are balanced, it is a BHUPP and the greatest results are achieved.

Labor Disputes and the BHUPP

The theory of the BHUPP shows its excellent explanatory power in the analysis of labor disputes. A labor dispute is a conflicting interest relationship between employee and employer, while at the same time it is a conflict between the vested interest and the challenger's interest. When the labor dispute is a conflicting relationship between employee and employer, it is a conflict between the private interest and the private interest. But if the labor dispute is a conflict between the vested interest and challenger's interest, it is a conflict between the private interest and the public interest. The interest of the laborer is a public interest of all the laborers, consisting of the private interests of each individual laborer; the interest of employer is a public interest, consisting of the private interests of each individual employer. The laborer's interest and the employer's interest are the public interest of the whole group of laborers or employers, but when they conflict between the laborer's interest and the employer's interest they act as a private interest. When the employer's interest and the laborer's interest unify, it becomes a public interest of the company. When this company's public interest opposes the public interest of another company, it acts as a private interest; when the interests of two companies combine, it becomes a greater public interest. Therefore, the public interest contains the private interest and the private interest contains the public interest. The complex combination of the private interest and the public interest appears as either a private or public interest.

The laborer's interest and the employer's interest have the meet and part relationship. The first unification of the laborer's interest and the employer's interest is the foundation of the company. If the laborer's interest and the employer's interest unify harmoniously and both interests increase, the company grows. If the results of growth are distributed fairly to the employer and laborer, then there will be harmony in the company; if they are distributed unfairly, then there will be discord in the company. If the laborer's interest and the employer's interest conflict continuously and fail to unify, both sides would lose the interest and the company would stop growing. If the laborer's interest and the employer's interest separate completely, it means the end of the company. The laborer's interest and the employer's interest can conflict and oppose each other, and they can be analyzed separately, but one cannot consider the laborer's interest apart from the employer's interest and cannot take into account the employer's interest apart from the laborer's interest.

The character of a labor dispute varies according to the shape and the structure of the company. When the employer is a single capitalist and the labor is constructed from many laborers, the character of the labor dispute is different from one in which the employer is constructed from many capitalists and the labor is constructed with a few laborers.

Depending upon the whether the employer is a private person or a public person, the labor dispute has different characteristics. If the owner of the company is a public organ, the labor dispute is a conflict between the public interest and the private interest. But if the owner of the company is a private person, the labor dispute is the conflict between the private interest and the private interest. Usually, the employer and the company are treated the same and the private interest of the employer and the public interest of the company are treated the same. This is an incorrect premise. The capitalist invests the capital and the laborer supplies the labor at the founding of the company—the capitalist bears the investment costs and the laborer bears the cost of the labor, but the company bears no cost itself. The operator of the company can be either a capital investor or a hired laborer, so the employer and the operator are not always the same. In general, the capital investors become operators of the company—they hire the laborer, operate the company, and take the profits after the payment of wages. So there is confusion in the notion that the capital investor and the operator of the company and the company are the same. But if we precisely analyze the structure of company, then the employer and the operator of company, the capital investor, the owner, and the company are all different. Therefore, we have to define the capital investor, the laborer, and the company separately in order to analyze the labor dispute. The most ideal structure for the employee-employer relationship is one in which all the laborers invest equally in the foundation of the company. In such cases the employee's interest and the employer's interest accord completely, and the private interest of each laborer and the public interest of whole laborers accord completely.

The solution of the labor dispute lies in reaching the accorded interest of both employee and employer. If they reach agreement and unify at the accorded point, the company will operate normally and will grow; both employer's interest and laborer's interest will increase. When the employer's interest and the laborer's interest unify, and if the amount of both interests are equally balanced, the accomplishment will be bigger.

If the laborer's interest does not appear normally because the employer disturbs the aggregation process, or if the laborer's interest and employer's interest are unbalanced because the employer slights the laborer, or if the laborer's interest is excessively effected because the labor power pushes aside the employer's interest unilaterally, then the excessive private interest phenomenon (小過現象) arises: One side might gain the advantage, but it is not profitable for the whole company.

Finally, harmonious unification is the most reasonable unification. If both the employer and the laborer are satisfied with the agreement, they can unify without resistance, and enlarge the pie harmoniously.

The Relationship between Civilian and Government and the BHUPP

The relationship between the public sector and the private sector is a typical relationship between the public interest and the private interest because public sectors pursue the public interests and private sectors pursue the private interests.

The public officers carry out public duties and the civilians carry out private interests. Therefore, when public workers are faithful to their public duties and civilians are faithful to their private duties, government can operate effectively and orderly. The theory that public is public-like and private is private-like is a kind of a stability theory, like in the Chia Jen hexagram.

The Chia Jen hexagram shows that when each family member does his or her duty best at the proper position, the family can maintain its normal functionality for a long time. Bureaucracy is institutionalized in order to carry out public affairs, and the structure and function of bureaucracy is similar to the Chia Jen hexagram. Therefore, each member in the bureaucracy has to do his best at his duty. The public workers should be impartial in their public work and should not use public authority in order to pursue private interests. When bureaucracy is impartial, the people will trustingly follow the bureaucracy and a harmonious unification between the public sector and the private sector can be made. From this point of view, the relationship between the public sector and the private sector is a kind of system theory—when a system is stable, the system functions normally.

System theory is a kind of stability theory and is different from the theory of change. Even though the theory of stability emphasizes the stability of the system, change is inevitable in the construction and the destruction of the system. So the construction of the system is a unification of the public interest and the private interest; the continuing harmonious unification is the maintenance of the system. If the public workers persist in public interests and slight the private interests, or if the civilians persist in private interests and slight the public interests, the public interests and the private interests will go astray. If they fail to find the accorded point (agreement), the government will not function. If this condition continues, the government will collapse.

If the bureaucracy suppresses the people with too strong of an authority, the people will boycott the government and will try to overthrow the government. But if public workers are impartial in public affairs, people will trust the government and the public workers and the people will unify—the government will function well and human society will grow. And if public workers approach people in a humble manner and explain the public interest to them, people will be inspired and they will unify harmoniously. In this case, if the public interest and the private interest are balanced, the accomplishment will be greater.

As the analysis demonstrates, the BHUPP explains the relationship between public affairs and civilian affairs fairly well.

Chapter 6

Conclusion

The goal of this study is to examine the theory of change (Chou I or I Ching), to discover the principles of change resulting from those theories, and to investigate the development of the theory of political change according to the theory of change. In order to do that, the first step was to analyze and generalize the existing theories of political change. In the second step, the theory of change was summarized as six principles of change—the creation, the Yang Pien Yin Hua, the cycling order, the harmonious unification, the balance, and the stability. The third step was an attempt to correlate these principles to the theory of political change. The final step was an examination of the utility and the applicability of these theories in reality, while seeking to correct the failings of the existing theories or to supplement those theories.

The existing theories about political change are summarized as three types: modernization; conflict; and balance. Modernization theory is a kind of evolutionism. According to this theory, human society develops step-by-step toward the particular aimed society and the development of knowledge, transportation, and communication, along with industrialization and urbanization, lead the social changes. Thus, this modernization causes the political changes. The principle of the changing action is the conflict between conservatives and reformers, and the result of the change is the improvement of function through differentiation and specialization. Modernization theory is suitable in the analysis of the process of modernization and the structure of specialization, but is not suitable in explaining the dynamic relation of the political change and the retrogressive phenomenon.

The conflict theory is based on the theory of the struggle for existence and the dialectical principle. According to this theory, the destruction of the extant is the premise of development, the principle of the changing action is the struggle for existence or contradiction, and the result of change is advancement. These theories are suitable to explain the dynamic aspects of political change, but they also justify violent acts such as war, revolution, or *coup d'états*.

The balance theory is a system-preservation, macro-analysis theory which looks at a whole society as a single unit. According to this theory, the political system needs stability in order for the system to carry out its normal function. Balance among the elements within the political system is essential for stability. If that balance tilts, there is tendency for the system to seek equilibrium—the correcting behavior is the cause of change. The principle of the changing action is the conflict and contradiction among components within the system; the result of the change is the transference of the balancing point.

As an organic theory, balance theory explains the growth and the degeneration of the political structure under the balanced conditions. Because of the theory's emphasis on balance and stability, it is suitable to explain the structure, function, and growth of a system, but it is not adequate to explain the change of systems or revolutionary upheavals.The analysis of the Chou I started with the theory of Tai Chi and Yin Yang, the origin of Chou I. After the analysis of Tai Chi theory and the Ho Tu and Lo Shu theories, six principles of change were summarized. They are: the creation; the Yang Pien Yin Hua; the cycling order; the harmonious unification; the balance; and the stability. In order to extract the political theories from these principles, the social meanings of the Yin-Yang were pursued. The results show that the Yin has a nature of the private (the private mind and the private interest), while the Yang has a nature of the public (the public mind and the public interest). The theories of political change were developed by the substitution of these concepts of private and the public. Finally, the author chose the most reasonable pattern of political change among the new theories and applied it to a few political phenomena. As a result, the new model of political change (BHUPP) can clearly explain ideological conflicts, labor disputes, and relationships between the public sector and the private sector, and can also suggest reasonable ways of change and the reasonable direction of change.

Conclusion

When we view the theory system of the Chou I in light of western modernization theory, we see Chou I contains the theory of the growth and the theory of circulation. Chou I defined growth as the goal of the human society, treated growth as a favorable phenomenon, and defined the period of growth as a good period and the period of decline as a bad period.

If we see Chou I in the view of the theory of conflict, Chou I is a kind of dialectic theory. The creational function that is the origination, the opposition, and the unification of the Yin-Yang repeats, so it is a kind of dialectical change (but it is different from Hegel's dialectic). Hegel's theory is a process of the Thesis-Antithesis-Synthesis, while Chou I is the process of an Alternate Creation of the Yin-Yang—the Unification of the Yin-Yang. Therefore, the opposition of the Yin-Yang is different in character from the opposition of Hegel's theory. Chou I did not define the final goal of human society and appeared as naturalism, so it did not assert to accelerate change in order to quickly get to the final goal of human society.

If we look at Chou I in the view of the balance theory, the theory structure of the Chou I is an organic theory. The origination and unification of the Yin-Yang create human beings and raise human society. If human society grows, the social structure will grow, and the political structure will grow, too. But the principle of growth and decline do not change, so orderly change is possible. That is the stability and the balance. It used the same model to explain both the structure of the family and the structure of the government. The structure of the family can grow to the structure of the government, but the model does not change. This is a type of system. When the system is stable, it can function normally. So this theory system is a type of structural functionalism. If the structure functions vigorously in a favorable period, the system will grow; if the structure does not function during an unfavorable period, the structure will decline. Therefore, the theory system of Chou I is a theory system of change which insists on the orderly growth of human society in the stable system, and one that harmonizes change and stability.

There were a few important accomplishments of the study of political change through the Chou I. First, the goal of politics was met by the study of the theory of change. The theory of change defined growth as the goal of the human race, and it illuminated the direction and the method of growth—it suggested ways to do things justly and properly.

Second, the theory of change provided a theory that corrects the contradiction of the existing dialectical theory, whose theorists defined the final goal of human society and chose conflict and opposition as the way to fulfill that final goal. In doing so, they accelerated the struggle that most people, by their nature, hate. On the other hand, the theory of change insists upon creational development through harmonious unification, emphasizes the principle of naturalism, and pursues improvement through sincerity.

Third, the study of political change according to *Chou I* clearly suggested the way to solve ideological conflict. The study defined the weakness of totalitarianism and individualism as an excessive public interest phenomenon (大過現象), as an excessive private interest phenomenon (小過現象), and explained that both phenomena are not reasonable. It also suggested that the solution to the ideological problem is not exclusionism, but rather a balanced unification and offered a guide to the practical method for achieving that goal.

Fourth, the study of political change according to Chou I simplified the analysis of complicated political problems as they relate to the public and private interests, and also analyzed the core of politics' dynamics and suggested the method and the model of the dynamical analysis. Most political problems in modern society arise from the interest relationship, so these interests can be analyzed as either public or private. If political problems can be so analyzed, there will be certain accorded points for the balanced unification. This model is a great theory that can analyze not only the interest relationship between individuals but also the interest relationship among nations. This model is a synthetic theory system of political change that shows the things which have to be changed and the things which do not have to be changed, guides the right change and the wrong change, and suggests the right way of change that will best fit a particular situation.

Bibliography

Almond, Gabriel, and G. Bingham Powell, Jr. *Comparative Politics: A Developmental Approach*. Boston: Little Brown, 1966.
Bill, James A., and Robert L. Hardgrave, Jr. *Comparative Politics*. Columbus Ohio: Charles E. Merrill, 1973.
Black, C. E. *The Dynamics of Modernization*. New York: Harper & Row, 1966.
Brewer, Garry D., and Ronald D. Brunner. *Political Development and Change*. New York: The Free Press, 1975.
Chilcote, Ronald H. *The Theories of Comparative Politics*. Boulder, Colorado: Westview Press, 1981.
Coleman, James S. "The Development Syndrome: Differentiation-Equality-Capacity." Social Science Research Council *Crises and Sequences in Political Development*. New Jersey: Princeton University Press, 1971.
Coser, Lewis A. "Social Conflict and the Theory of Social Change," *British Journal of Sociology*, VII, Sept. 1957.
Dalton, Melville. "Conflicts Between Staff and Line Managerial Offices," *American Sociological Review*, XV, 3. Jun.1950.
Daniels, Robert V. *Marxism and Communism*. New York: Random House, 1967.
Deutsch, Karl. "Social Mobilization and Political Development." *American Political Science Review* 55, Sept. 1961.
Dewey, John. *Human Nature and Conduct*. New York: The Modern Library, 1930.
Eisenstadt, S. N. "Initial Institutional Patterns of Political Modernization." *Civilizations*, XII, No. 4 (1967).
Halpern, Manfred. "The Rate and Costs of Political Development." *Annals of the American Academy of Political and Social Science*, 358, No. 1. Princeton: University Press, 1965.

Herberg, Will. "The Study of Man: When Social Scientists View Labor." *Community*, XI, Dec. 1951.
Hofstadter, Richard. *Social Darwinism In American Thought 1860-1915*. Philadelphia: The University of Philadelphia Press, 1944.
Huntington, Samuel P. *Political Order in Changing Society*. New Haven: Yale University Press, 1968.
———. "Political Development and Political Decay," *World Politics* XVII, April 1965.
Kaemfert, Waldemar. "Science in Review." *The New York Times*. July 27, 1952.
Lerner, Max. "Vested Interest." *Encyclopaedia of the Social Sciences*. XV. London: Routledge, 1996.
Marx, Karl. *Early Writings*. New York: McGraw-Hill, 1964.
Marx, Karl, and Friedrich Engels. *The Communist Manifesto*. London: C. Nicholls & Co. Ltd, 1976.
Mazrui, Ali A. "From Social Darwinism to Current Theories of Modernization: A Traditional Analysis," *World Politics*, 21. Baltimore: Johns Hopkins University Press, Oct.1968.
Melman, Seymour. *Dynamic Factors in Industrial Productivity*. New York: Wiley, 1956.
Mitchell, William C. *The American Polity*, Glencoe, New York: The Free Press, 1962.
Morgenthau, Hans J. *Politics Among Nations*, New York: Alfred A. Knopf, 1978.
Muller, F. Max. *The I Ching*. New York: Dover Publications, 1899.
Pye, Lucian, *Aspects of Political Development*. Boston: Little Brown, 1966.
Riggs, Fred W. "The Dialectics of Developmental Conflicts," *Comparative Political Studies* I, July 1968. Reprinted in Robert Jackson and Michael Stein, eds. *Issues in Comparative Politics*. New York: St. Martin's Press, 1971.
Rustow, Dankwart A. "Change as the Theme of Political Science," in Chalmers Johnson, ed., *Change in Communist Systems*. California: Stanford University Press, 1970.
Sanders, David. *Patterns of Political Instability*. New York: St. Martin's Press, 1980.
Sorel, Georges. *Reflections on Violence*. New York: B.W. Huebsch, 1915.

Steinbruner, John D. *The Cybernetic Theory of Decision.* New Jersey: Princeton University Press, 1976.
Straus, Leo, and Joseph Cropsy. *History of Political Philosophy.* Chicago: The University of Chicago Press, 1981.
Veblem, Thorstein. *The Vested Interests and the State of the Industrial Arts.* New York: B.W. Huebsch, 1919.
Wilhelm, Hellmut. *The I Ching: Book of Changes.* New Jersey: Princeton University Press, 1967.

姜天奉, "啓蒙傳疑硏究", 退溪學報 第十六輯, 서울：退溪學硏究院, 1977. pp.124~130.

姜天奉, "啓蒙傳疑硏究", 退溪學報 第十七輯, 서울：退溪學硏究院, 1978. pp.95~116.

金學俊, 現代政治過程論, 서울：法文社, 1978.

金赫濟, 原本集註 周易, 서울：明文堂, 1987.

金赫濟, 原本備旨 大學·中庸, 서울：明文堂, 1986.

南晚星, 論語, 서울：瑞文堂, 1981.

孟華燮, 周易講議, 大邱漢醫科大學,

沈鍾哲, 周易, 서울：大韓曆法硏究所, 1979.

安耕田, 개벽, 서울：大原出版社, 1988.

李家源, 大學·中庸, 서울：弘新文化社, 1985.

李民樹, 孟子, 서울：瑞文堂, 1978.

李民樹, 詩經, 서울：正音社, 1976.

李民樹, 書經, 서울：瑞文堂, 1976.

李相殷, 聖學十圖譯解, 서울：退溪學硏究院, 1982.

李相殷, 退溪의 生涯와 學問, 서울：瑞文堂, 1978.

韓東錫, 宇宙變化의 原理, 서울：행림출판사, 1985.

鈴木由次郞, 易經, 東京：集英社, 昭和49年.

張立文, "朱熹與李滉的易學思想比較硏究", 退溪學報, 第43輯, 1984.

張立文, "李退溪哲學邏集結構深析", 退溪學報, 第45輯, 1985.

姜天奉, "啓蒙傳疑硏究", 退溪學報 第三輯, 서울 : 退溪學硏究院, 1974. pp.76~133.

姜天奉, "啓蒙傳疑硏究", 退溪學報 第四輯, 서울 : 退溪學硏究院, 1974. pp.79~143.

姜天奉, "啓蒙傳疑硏究", 退溪學報 第五·六輯, 서울 : 退溪學硏究院, 1975. pp.170~231.

姜天奉, "啓蒙傳疑硏究", 退溪學報 第七輯, 서울 : 退溪學硏究院, 1975. pp.97~145.

姜天奉, "啓蒙傳疑硏究", 退溪學報 第九輯, 서울 : 退溪學硏究院, 1975. pp.89~117.

姜天奉, "啓蒙傳疑硏究", 退溪學報 第十輯, 서울 : 退溪學硏究院, 1976. pp.136~148.

姜天奉, "啓蒙傳疑硏究", 退溪學報 第十一輯, 서울 : 退溪學硏究院, 1976. pp.106~112.

姜天奉, "啓蒙傳疑硏究", 退溪學報 第十二輯, 서울 : 退溪學硏究院, 1976. pp.65~103.

姜天奉, "啓蒙傳疑硏究", 退溪學報 第十三輯, 서울 : 退溪學硏究院, 1977. pp.107~115.

姜天奉, "啓蒙傳疑硏究", 退溪學報 第十四輯, 서울 : 退溪學硏究院, 1977. pp.216~231.

姜天奉, "啓蒙傳疑硏究", 退溪學報 第十五輯, 서울 : 退溪學硏究院, 1977. pp.118~128.

www.ingramcontent.com/pod-product-compliance
Lightning Source LLC
Chambersburg PA
CBHW030114010526
44116CB00005B/241